THE
WOW
FACTOR

ALSO BY FRANCES COLE JONES

How to Wow

THE
WOW
FACTOR

The 33 Things You Must (and Must Not)
Do to Guarantee Your Edge in Today's
Business World

FRANCES COLE JONES

Ballantine Books Trade Paperbacks
New York

2010 Ballantine Books Trade Paperback Edition

Copyright © 2009 by Frances Cole Jones

All rights reserved.

Published in the United States by Ballantine Books, an imprint of The Random
House Publishing Group, a division of Random House, Inc., New York.

BALLANTINE and colophon are registered trademarks of Random House, Inc.

Originally published in hardcover in the United States by Ballantine Books, an
imprint of The Random House Publishing Group, a division of Random House,
Inc., in 2009.

Library of Congress Cataloging-in-Publication Data

Jones, Frances Cole.
   The wow factor : the 33 things you must (and must not) do to guarantee
your edge in today's business world / Frances Cole Jones.
      p. cm.
ISBN 978-0-345-51793-7
1. Success in business.   I. Title.
HF5386.J777 2009
658.4'09—dc22   2009029838

Printed in the United States of America

www.ballantinebooks.com

9 8 7 6 5 4 3 2 1

Book design by Diane Hobbing of Snap-Haus Graphics

This book is dedicated to the memory of Sri K. Pattabhi Jois, with everlasting gratitude and joy

To
Milo Logan Jones,
the consummate Renaissance man,
and Debra Goldstein,
the Consigliere of Wow

Contents

Introduction

On April 29, 2008, *How to Wow* was published to a gratifying reception—shortly afterward, the world as we knew it collapsed. The recession, or "credit crunch," had arrived.

Within days my phone was ringing off the hook: Clients who had suddenly been "outsourced," and clients desperate to keep the jobs they had, were looking for answers.

This is when my company kicked it up to Code Orange—my clients needed cutting-edge information, and they needed it immediately. (Trust me, when you get a call from a CEO's family saying he's on suicide watch, you don't reply with "Let me check my calendar.") They needed solutions, skills, and tactics—yesterday.

This is how *The Wow Factor* was born.

The Wow Factor offers thirty-three things you absolutely must *and absolutely must not* do to survive in today's business world. From corporate CEOs who suddenly need to reinvent themselves, to recent graduates facing unprecedented, fierce competition, to entrepreneurs who need to secure funding when funding is seemingly nonexistent, to those wondering if the industry they're working in will continue to exist—I've coached them all, and more. These proven tools can give you the edge you need to recession-proof your job—no, make that your career.

And because it's likely many of you are in the same position as my recent clients, there's going to be far less sugarcoating this time around. They needed shortcuts. And—if you're like one of the many people I know walking around with their stomachs in knots and their insomnia in overdrive—I'm guessing you do too.

What kinds of skills am I talking about? Everything from how to restore your confidence—critical in these days of "Look hungry, go hungry"—to how to outprepare your interviewer, to how to leverage your network when the last thing you want to do is pick up the phone one more time.

This world demands creativity, fluidity, and persistence the likes of which few of us have had to call on before. *The Wow Factor* provides resources and answers.

And for those of you who are thinking you might just use this time to keep your head down and avoid the shrapnel, I'd like to point out that the widget you're intent on continuing to make will likely not be needed by this brave new world—nor will anyone have the money to buy it. (Should you doubt this, please note that a study done by Digital Ethnography states that when the majority of today's college students graduate they will be applying for jobs that don't currently exist because the technology hasn't yet been invented.)

Another important consideration is how much opportunity turbulent times provide for those with the guts and skill to seize it. One of my best clients runs a business her grandfather founded during the depths of the Great Depression. He took a big risk, and three generations later, she and her customers benefit from the determination, optimism, and vision he showed in 1936.

With this in mind, then, how can you evolve, change, and survive in a time when corporations we held as bulletproof are gone? Lehman Brothers and Bear Stearns are gone. General Motors and AIG are teetering. What's next?

What's next is you at the top of your game. The tools I offered in *How to Wow* were basic, and basic is no longer enough. Basic is now merely mandatory.

In the interest of getting you where you needed to be yesterday, I kept *How to Wow*'s "search and destroy" format and divided *The Wow Factor* into three sections: Practice, Know, and Do.

Section One: Practice looks at the attitudes, habits, and skills that will enable you to feel calm, confident, and in command from *within*, so you can project these qualities to an increasingly turbulent outside world. Internalizing these principles and disciplines alters your mental wiring in such a way that the self-confidence you project comes from the self-esteem you've embraced, a shift that is critical to an authentic external presentation. In these days when "buyer beware" is uppermost in everyone's minds—when anyone with the faintest whiff of uneasiness, unctuousness, or inability is the first to face the firing line—this is not a choice.

Section Two: Know includes information vital to getting along in today's world, offering everything I've learned about how to effectively target your dream job, get your résumé to the top of the pile, outprepare your interviewer, and thrive once you've landed the position you want. It will also look at the many ways we communicate in writing (text, email, snail mail) and the situations in which we do (responding to interested employers, setting up meetings and interviews, posting social networking profiles) and shows you how to express yourself clearly, accurately, and elegantly in every scenario. In this economy, mastery of technological media is no longer enough. Expressing yourself memorably, *and* with grace, via every line of communication you use, is a must. This section also addresses the value of play, silence, and circumlocution, and the necessity of packing a verbal one-two punch. To succeed in your communication, sometimes you want to stand out and sometimes you want to fit in. This section ensures your skill, whichever you intend.

Finally, **Section Three: Do** outlines the action steps necessary to make things happen, whether this is building your own advisory board, making your expectations explicit, adopting the number one rule for a successful job search ("Do It, Delegate It, or Delete It"), keeping at the forefront of technology, building trust, leveraging your existing network, or adding to it. You will also learn to barter your skills and connections in such a way that whether you need inside information on tomorrow's business lunch, a spot on the guest list at a sales prospect's party, or a website redesign in exchange for a wardrobe overhaul, you know who to call, and how to get results once you have that person on the phone. In short, this section tells you how to guarantee that the largely internal and personal changes described in Sections One and Two make an impact on the real world.

Throughout, *The Wow Factor* offers sample scripts and sidebars to give you practical, factual ways to implement this information without delay. Each section will also conclude with a bulleted "top line message" list of what was included.

Most important, however, *The Wow Factor* offers you the certainty of knowing that your ideas and skills are both up-to-the-minute and timeless, ensuring that regardless of your current situation—and no matter how high your future goals—your edge over your competition is guaranteed.

And that edge is the wow factor.

THE
WOW
FACTOR

SECTION ONE
PRACTICE

In sports, the ability to shave a hundredth of a second off your time can be what determines the difference between the gold and the silver medal. In turbulent economic times, the same is true—getting the job, the deal, the account is determined by the smallest of degrees.

How, then, can you ensure you're standing on the winning platform? The same way athletes do: by developing the habits, skills, and disciplines that will stand you in good stead, regardless of the state of the playing field. And in the same way their training routines and practices are designed to leave nothing to chance, you must ensure that your habits keep you in the best shape possible.

When you're called into the game, you need to be at the top of your game.

What are some of the qualities that dull your edge? Everything from the seemingly innocuous unexamined habit, through disorganization and trepidation, all the way to the flat-out fear that paralyzes your thinking, not to mention your ability to act in your own best interest. For myself, I know that when I'm off my game I tend to adopt the coping skills of Lucy Ricardo—changing what might have been a manageable situation into an operatic showdown at Club Babalu.

Given this, over the years I've developed, discovered, and learned from the brightest stars with whom I work a number of ideas, habits, and tools that help me present my best self regardless of the circumstances. For example, I've learned how to actively create camaraderie in meetings, strategically choose projects that guarantee the biggest bang for my buck, and consciously create customer satisfaction along the entire chain of my business.

The tips and tools offered in this section, then, are things you must do to fine-tune how you show up every day—mental weight lifting, if you will. And, in the same way those seemingly pointless bicep curls and leg presses you do in the gym ensure you the necessary physical strength to carry your kids to safety if your house is on fire, these tips and tools ensure you the mental strength you'll need when your interview gets moved from tomorrow to today, your colleagues are gunning for your job, or your boss has been asked to put together his "early retirement" short list. Armed with up-to-the-minute technical acumen and finely honed people skills, you'll be poised to instead grab that promotion.

1 | Retrain Your Brain

"That's one small step for man . . ." Most of you are likely able to finish Neil Armstrong's sentence regarding his first step on the moon: ". . . one giant leap for mankind."

I propose that mental strength, and its twin brother, confidence, are gained in much the same way. While I am intent on avoiding the obvious Lao-tzu quote (journey/thousand miles/single step/etc.), I think the sentiment is one it's important to remember. Circumnavigating, removing, or changing your attitude toward the obstacles you currently face is far more manageable if you break it down into discrete steps. And the fact is that even small changes begin to retrain your brain. This phenomenon, called "neuroplasticity," is a burgeoning field in brain research, and thanks to the latest brain scanning technology, it is increasingly clear that adults can—and do—sharpen their brains, heal learning problems, and more.

In short, you can teach yourself resilience.

Should you be skeptical, here's an immediate, tangible example of simple brain retraining: Stop reading this and interlace your fingers. Now, unlace them and relace with your other index finger on top.

If you are like most people this switch will feel awfully peculiar. The reason for this is that we generally interlace our fingers with the index finger of our dominant hand on top—it's our body's habit. And, like so many habits, we accept it without question. But, as has been pointed out to me, your habits are your destiny—and would you accept your destiny without lifting a finger to change it?

What other small physical habits might you look at? Well, you might notice if you always step out of the shower or start down the stairs with the same foot first, or brush your teeth or throw a ball with the same hand. If you do, switch it up. Research has shown that doing so stimulates the production of brain-derived neurotrophic factor, a protein that plays a critical role in the regulation of metabolism, immune reactions, and stress responses—a small price to pay to support your body's efforts to maintain its weight, stay healthy, and remain calm.

How can you apply this information to your work life? My request is that you pick one thing—one thing only—that you want to change and focus on that for a month. If you have a habit of putting off making cold calls because you dread both the research and the rejection, I want you to pick one person or company that you've mentally targeted and rather than give yourself the goal of getting to them *today*, tell yourself that today is just the day you are going to do the research: find out as much as you can about their background and then write down all the ways in which your skill set can improve their life or business. Tomorrow, I would ask that you write down every possible objection they might have to your suggestions, and how you might counter those objections. For example, if someone were to say, "I don't have the budget," your response might be "The meeting's free." Time on day three could be spent researching the gatekeepers and deciding what methods of persuasion are most likely to gain you access. Day four you might make the call, and day five send your follow-up email or letter.

Now, you might be thinking, "I don't have a week to make one phone call—I need things to change *now*." Perhaps, but it's that kind of thinking that causes people to feel overwhelmed, which generally leads to dread and avoidance. Breaking the challenge down into concrete steps and taking charge of each in a methodical way automatically makes you feel more in control.

So, back to cold calls: Week two, I'd want you to target job or person number two. I'm guessing that by now you'll be quicker at each step—you might even find you look forward to the challenge, and will get two calls in. By week three you could be on a roll, making up to three calls. At the end of the month, it will be a new habit. And while this may not seem groundbreaking in the abstract, doing just one new thing a month guarantees that by the end of the year you will have adopted twelve new habits—which is, I think, the equivalent of one giant leap.

2 | Look for Angels Wearing Overalls

Thomas Edison told us, "The reason that so few people recognize opportunity is that it comes dressed in overalls and looks a lot like hard work." This idea is vital to networking, where an invitation can so often seem like a waste of time, or a request can feel like an underutilization of our skills—not to mention not jibing with where we feel we should be in our careers.

That said, I can state unequivocally that some of the most extraordinary clients I've worked with have been the result of connections I made doing pro bono lectures—and not just pro bono: pro bono in a remote location at an unspeakable hour of the morning. I recently picked up some of my most lucrative, ongoing work from agreeing to make myself available for an initial small, somewhat absurd, request: talking to an A-list celebrity on the telephone for fifteen minutes about what she planned to say during her star turn at a major midtown Manhattan Christmas event. The ongoing work for which I've since been contracted will see me through the coming year.

Similarly, I have found that some of the most valuable experience I've gained has come from doing jobs and learning skills that didn't initially seem worth my time. For example, when I was working in publishing, I made a point of taking both copyediting and proofreading classes, despite the fact that, as an acquisitions editor, neither of these skills was integral to my job. Why, then, was this information useful? Because it gave me instant credibility with the copyeditors and proofreaders I worked alongside; I understood their language, constraints, and needs, which meant that when I needed a favor—extra time with a manuscript, extra patience with an author—they were more likely to accede. All of which improved my standing with those at the top.

As Samuel Goldwyn said, "I find that the harder I work, the more luck I seem to have."

How, then, can you begin to recognize when the knock at the door is, in fact, opportunity? One way is to broaden your definition of your job—to examine your knee-jerk reaction that thus-and-such is beneath you. Are there skill sets within your industry that others have but you haven't acquired? Steps in the chain of production you don't have a grasp on? Internal communication processes you haven't bothered to examine, much less master? Getting in the trenches with regard to this knowledge will not only make you more effective at your job, it will make you a more effective leader: The people working for you will know that not only can you talk the talk, you can walk the walk. Two of my most successful—and well-liked—CEOs are so effective because they took the time to understand the ins and outs of their rank-and-file employees' days. One, a retail magnate, set himself to work folding sweaters at a major department store during the holiday rush; the other, the CEO of a food services giant, learned how to drive the eighteen-wheelers his team was using to transport his products coast to coast. Not only did both find their experiences helpful to their understanding of their company, they found them invaluable for building credibility and morale.

Another thing I recommend you do is accept networking invitations, regardless of how useless or uninviting the prospect of attending might seem. After all, sitting in front of the television or seeing the same old crowd is not exactly putting yourself in the path of serendipity. (The term "serendipity," by the way, was coined by the writer Horace Walpole after reading a fairy tale, "The Three Princes of Serendip"; these princes "were always making discoveries, by accident or sagacity, of things they were not in quest of.") In this regard, networking is much like dating: Most dates you go on don't end in happily-ever-after. That said, as with dating, you aren't going to meet Mr. or Ms. Right by going straight from your office to the gym/your local restaurant/your TV and an order of takeout. If nothing else, attending networking events is critical for the practice you get networking—so that when you do meet the connection of your dreams, you have on your game face.

3 | Create Camaraderie

We've all had the experience of sitting through an awkward meeting, lunch, or phone call — one that, no matter how hard we try, never seems to get off the ground. While there is no scientific formula for making these moments work, there are a number of tools you can use to both prepare yourself for success and ensure your polished follow-up:

Pick Three Small-Talk Topics:

While it may seem a bit pedantic, it's often helpful to think through three potential topics for small talk prior to your arrival. In my experience it's best to choose from a fairly broad range of possibilities: say, sports, movies, and — depending on the crowd — local restaurants or attractions that you have researched. What this does is smooth over transitional moments such as waiting for the last participant to arrive for the meeting, for the waiter to bring your menus, or for the elevator when you're ready to leave — all of which can be awkward if silent, or potentially deal-breaking if the topic you choose at random lands badly with your listeners.

Eat and Drink What You're Offered:

This is something many people have asked me about — their concern being that if they accept an offer of water, coffee, or drinks or food of any kind, they are being difficult or demanding. In fact, accepting hospitality signals both your openness to the other person and your feelings regarding a potentially positive outcome to the meeting as a whole. This doesn't mean that if you're offered coffee you say, "May I have a double no-fun, no-foam mochachino with six Splendas." All that's necessary is "Yes, thank you." If you're worried about nerves, I recommend water over coffee, as—caffeine intake issues aside—water's likely to come in a tumbler, which, depending on the design, is probably easier to manage than a coffee cup. I include this quite specifically, as one of my clients told me he once accepted an offer of coffee and then found that his hands were shaking too badly to pick it up. If you do somehow manage to spill your drink in every direction (as I have done), don't panic. Ask where paper towels are, help with the cleanup, apologize once, and move on.

Write Down What People Tell You:

Because I have a freakish ability to retain what's said to me without writing it down, I rarely, if ever, used to take notes in meetings. What I discovered from one of my clients is that this made him very, very nervous. If he didn't see me writing it down, he didn't believe I was going to remember it. Having consequently made a habit of doing this, I've noticed that it both frees others up mentally—the same way it does when you see your waiter or waitress write down your order—and gives them a sense they have actively contributed, which improves morale all around. With this in mind, whether you use the notes or not, write down what others tell you.

Make Notes Immediately Upon Leaving:

One of my most successful financial clients makes a point of jotting down notes on any personal information mentioned immediately upon leaving a meeting or lunch. This allows him, in his thank-you note, to be very specific with his follow-up—for example, "It was so wonderful to hear Jane and Sally are doing so well in school," or "I do hope Tom enjoys his time at camp this summer." The PR executive with whom I most enjoy working likely does the same (and it's one of the many reasons I so enjoy her): I've noted that she never fails to ask how my dog is, and it never ceases to make me smile.

Ensure Communication Flows:

In addition to making yourself available to those with whom you meet, you should ensure that your staff is able to do the same. This means that anytime you're going to be out of the office for an extended period of time, they are told how and where to reach you. They should also have the names of all current and potential clients in hand, and a general idea of the status of every project, so they can say with authority, "Hello, Mr. X. No, he's not in the office at the moment, but I know he's been wanting to speak with you. Here is how to reach him," or, "Hello, Mr. X. No, he's not in the office at the moment. I know you're calling him about Y project. Is there something that I can help you with immediately?" Either response is guaranteed to leave the listener feeling he or she is valuable to your team.

As you can see, while none of the above is groundbreaking in itself, each creates a sense of camaraderie and community within a business environment, both of which are just short steps from the trust that's needed to seal the deal.

4 | Offer Others an All-Access Pass

Few things are as off-putting as asking someone to exchange information with you, only to have them give you their office's main number and their assistant's extension. Similarly, if and when you are asked for your information, it's important to be generous. I'm not suggesting you hand over your home telephone number, but I am saying that in this day and age, it's easy enough to give people several ways to reach you: cellphone, Skype number, email, etc.

This approach is also a form of politeness—implicit in it is that people prefer different modes of communication. I always offer people at least two ways to contact me, and mention which one works best for me. If you're highly mobile—across time zones or continents, I mean—this multimethod contact tactic is crucial, as it makes others' lives more convenient and keeps your cellphone from going off at 4 A.M. (or worse, keeps people from wondering why you sound like you just woke up at 11 A.M.).

Do I have specific suggestions with regard to other elements of your business card? Not surprisingly, I do. And while there are as many permutations of business cards as there are businesses—and there are no hard-and-fast rules about what is "acceptable" and what isn't—I'd like to offer the following list of recommendations:

1. Have them. Regardless of whether or not you are currently employed by a firm, you should have business cards that state your full name and complete contact information.

2. As discussed, include multiple ways to reach you: landline, cell, Skype number, email, snail mail address. You don't want the card to look cluttered, but you do want to give people confidence that you can be reached—and that you're in step with modern technology.

3. If you aren't employed by a firm, and the holder of a particular title, I'd prefer that you not include a description of what you do, because while you may indeed be a writer, editor, agent, or producer, there's a whiff of desperation in including that on your card.

4. I don't recommend including slogans, mission statements, affirmations, inspirational sayings, etc.

5. If your company's logo is easily incorporated into the card, then by all means include it. If it's unwieldy, I'd leave it off. If you're creating your own cards, I'd prefer you not include any design elements on offer at your local printing shop. You're unique. Your card should be too.

6. That said, unless it is your profession, I'd proceed with caution in creating a design element of your own. Given the number of variables in play—scale, color, its interaction with typeface—it's far better to have your personal "brand identity" professionally created.

7. I'm not a fan of unusual trim sizes. Slightly larger or square can make it difficult for others to fit it in their wallets. Slightly smaller can come across as precious.

8. Don't skimp on your paper quality. Yes, it's an additional expense to have cards printed on heavy stock, but it makes them far more memorable (and durable) for the receiver.

Why do these do's and don'ts matter so much? Because ultimately your card is selling you, and in this business environment you need something whose information and quality of design and printing are a direct reflection of the value you offer.

If you find yourself in a situation where you've forgotten your card, rather than scrawling your information on the back of a napkin or piece of scrap paper, I would ask the person you're meeting with if he or she has a spare and then write your information on the back of that—we often throw out old scraps of paper when cleaning our wallets, but we're unlikely to throw out our own business cards, so there's less of a possibility your details will land in the trash.

In Japan, the custom when handing others your card is to hold it with two hands and bow when it's offered. While I don't think it's necessary to go to that extreme, I also don't want a handoff that looks like you're doing a drug deal (something I see a lot), one that includes furtive glances at surrounding people on the part of the giver and studied nonchalance on the part of the receiver. When you take another's card—regardless of the value you perceive it offers—you need to treat it as valuable. Make a point of putting it into your wallet or purse. Thrusting it into the pocket of your suit can leave the giver thinking he's more likely to get a call from your dry cleaner than from you.

Although the World Wide Web allows us to stay in touch with one another in numerous ways, the business card is not going out of fashion anytime soon. Taking the time to incorporate these recommendations and habits into your routine ensures that when you do find yourself offering your contact data to people with whom you'd love to connect, they will be able to find you.

5 | Don't Work in a Goat's Stomach

When I was working in the nine-to-five world, there was a gentleman down the hall whose office inevitably looked like it had been stirred up with a stick: a desk loaded with piles of paper, dirty cups, take-out containers, a Magic 8 Ball, and a keyboard that looked like you'd better be wearing a hazmat suit when you touched it; more piles of papers on the desk, on the floor, on the chairs; shelving that was loaded with books, photos, and (bizarrely) pieces of sporting equipment; various items of clothing tossed hither and yon—jackets, sweaters, socks, shoes, hats. . . . One day, our boss walked by and said, "That office looks like the inside of a goat's stomach."

Not surprisingly, the occupant of the messy office wasn't with the company much longer.

What I've learned since then is that my colleague had created a petri dish of the three kinds of recognized office clutter. As identified by psychologist Sam Gosling, they are "identity clutter": photos of family, friends, pets, etc., that are designed to remind us we have a life outside the office; "thought and feeling regulators," which are chosen to change our mood (squeezable stress balls, miniature Zen gardens, daily affirmation calendars) and "behavior residues"—old coffee cups, food wrappers, Post-its stuck to the keyboard, etc.

The trouble with having a disproportionate number of these items in and around your office is that it sends a message to those around you that you are out of control. As one of my CEO clients said to me after we'd walked past his junior report's disastrously messy office on our way to his company's conference room, "Doesn't she realize I notice—and care?"

Now I'm not saying you can't have a few personal items. (And I am certainly not going to mandate, as one of my clients has done, what kinds of flowers you are allowed to receive. In that office, your loved ones can send you a white orchid. That's it.) But I am saying it's important to choose carefully, cull frequently, and clean daily.

In an effort to help you decide what stays and what goes, I have put together two lists: Remove Immediately and Keep Selectively. Given its urgency, let's first look at those items I'd prefer you remove immediately:

Remove Immediately:

- Leftover food; food wrappers; dirty cups, plates, or silverware. While this may seem self-evident, I imagine that more than a few of you have found yourself at five o'clock speaking to your coworkers from amid a small forest of half-empty coffee cups. (And I'm hoping there are at least one or two of you who—like me—are still drinking absentmindedly from your 8 A.M. coffee at 5 P.M., a practice I'm prone to if not carefully supervised, which always makes my assistant exclaim with disgust.) All of these must go—again, if you're like me, for your own sake if no one else's. When you do remove them, please don't simply dump them in the sink of the shared kitchen down the hall. I know of one office that based its recent decision as to which of two equally qualified and experienced people was laid off on who was more prone to leaving their dirty dishes in the communal kitchen; deciding factors these days are, indeed, this small.

- Dead flowers/plants. The roses your ex gave you last Valentine's Day shouldn't become a dried flower arrangement on the shelf. That shedding ficus tree will be much happier if given to a friend with a green thumb.

- Stuffed animals/"whimsical" toys (such as the aforementioned Magic 8 Ball). While these can be helpful should your—or your

boss's—kids come to the office, day to day they have the potential to undermine others' perceptions of the professionalism you
bring to your work.

Keep Selectively:

- Grooming products. Hairbrushes, toothbrushes/paste, shaving
  and nail paraphernalia can all be handy to have on hand. Please
  don't, however, leave them in plain sight—or perform any
  personal maintenance in front of others.

- Extra pairs of shoes/a shirt. Again, both are useful on days when
  you have an unexpectedly important meeting, or uncooperative
  weather. They should, however, be stowed out of others' sight
  lines.

- Photos of family/friends. While these are lovely reminders of
  your life outside the office and can be great conversation
  starters, please do make sure everyone in each photo is fully
  clothed and behaving appropriately. . . .

All this said, I do know that an office has to be worked in—and
that worrying about keeping it pristine can, ultimately, detract from
focusing on what you need to accomplish. For this reason, it can help
to set aside fifteen minutes at the middle and end of each day to clear
your desk/chairs/floor of any accumulated clutter. A principle applied by airlines and luxury bus lines, these intermittent sweeps help
keep things from piling up.

Having dealt with personal items, I'd like to speak briefly about
the ways in which people organize their work, because while some
people find it easy to keep their "to do" list on one sheet of paper,
their in- and out-boxes tidy, and their piles of papers (loosely)
aligned, others are sparked by visual reminders of what needs to get
done, resulting in multiple Post-its affixed to desktops and computer
screens, project folders piled on corners of desks, and stacks of papers

on the floor like a trail of Hansel and Gretel's bread crumbs. For these people, putting things in drawers is, in fact, disastrous, as it's "Out of sight, out of mind." If this is the case for you, I would recommend buying two wire-rack step files for your desk: one for current projects and one for "to do" items. This keeps the things you need in plain sight but ensures that the top of your desk isn't chaotic. You might also organize two rows of items on one side of your desk, with those that are most time-sensitive at the front.

As you can see, the phrase "Look good, feel good" is one that can and should be applied to your office as well as your person, and although it can be troubling in a wholly different way to see a row of color-coded thumbtacks aligned on someone's bulletin board, if you're presenting a chaotic, dirty shop front to the world, it's hard for those around you to believe in the quality of the work you can, or will, produce.

"I Wondered Where That Was. . . ."

Lisa Zaslow, founder and CEO of Gotham Organizers (www.gotham-organizers.com), was kind enough to send me the following list of items found in various clients' office spaces in the last six months. Suffice it to say, if you have any of these lying about, I would remove them posthaste:

- a 20-pound box of oatmeal
- dozens of bottle caps from Poland Spring water
- a pharmacy's worth of aspirin, allergy medicines, nose spray, throat lozenges, etc.
- Phone books, journals, newspapers, Zagats, catalogs, etc., that are years old (doesn't make you look very up-to-date)
- tons of giveaways from trade shows and conferences—stress balls, tote bags, portfolios, clocks, pedometers, pads, pens, picture frames, etc.
- cases of wine

- bottles of liquor
- framed art on the floor; crumpled posters
- ratty cardboard boxes of marketing materials, books, T-shirts from company events, sample products, banners, etc.
- banker's boxes of old papers stacked in corners
- boxes of office supplies
- old computers, phones, Palm Pilots, printers, TVs
- the packing materials and instruction booklets for all these old computers, phones, Palm Pilots, printers, and TVs
- cables, wires, cords, and more cables
- bags of stuff that you've been intending to bring home (but that have been sitting in your office for years)
- unopened bags of stuff you've forgotten you purchased or received as gifts—office supplies, pen sets, candy, clothes, you name it
- coins, clips, pens, papers, and other items scattered around the surface of the desk so there is no room for work
- windowsills and bookcases filled with all of the above
- and, of course, piles and piles and piles of papers—covering every horizontal surface, available seat, the floor . . .

Home Office Professionalism

More and more people are self-employed or otherwise working from a home office. Given this, here are a few ways to ensure that you always appear professional (and some tips for improving your efficiency):

1. If you don't already know, learn how to make address labels on your home printer—hand-addressed mail looks less official.
2. Similarly, get an online postage account or a postal machine (see www.stamps.com or www.pitneyworks.com). Franked mail looks more businesslike than multiple stamps, and the Pitney Bowes Personal Post machine even lets you add small corporate messages to your postmark.

3. If you do use stamps, be sure they are appropriate—e.g., don't send something to a client with a "Season's Greetings" stamp in August, or a "Love" stamp just because the post office is pushing them around Valentine's Day.

4. If you don't have a fax at home, get a free fax number online: There are a lot of deals out there, but www.efax.com has a good basic service for nothing.

5. Set up an individual FedEx account—it makes sending overnight packages much easier, and all you need to do it is a credit card.

6. If you're working on a big project, you can easily "expand" the size of your office by incorporating the Post-it Tabletop Easel Pad; these whiteboard-sized Post-its are a great way to give a conference-room-sized feel to a closet-sized office.

7. A "countdown clock" is a great way to ensure you stay on task. Used for everything from planning weddings to planning conferences, numerous models are available at www.alibaba.com.

8. Consider a separate phone line, especially if you have kids.

9. Sometimes people have trouble believing that you actually *work* from home—they think that because you're at home, you're free. To reinforce this boundary, I recommend:
   - You get caller ID.
   - Start conversations when you're working at home with "What can I do for you?" as opposed to "How are you?"
   - Rehearse a few phrases you can use to move the conversation along. For example, "Oh, hi—I'm working on a tight deadline (just in the middle of finishing a project, etc.). May I call you back tonight?"

10. Home offices can make you a little peculiar after a while—if you're not careful, it's awfully easy to begin spending the day in your pajamas. Given this, I recommend establishing routines for working on major projects, returning emails, even getting out in the world. In keeping with the Renaissance attitude advocated next, you might even get yourself a one-year pass to the local botanical garden or museum if it's nearby, and make use of it when you want to give yourself time to step away and regroup.

6 | Adopt a Renaissance Attitude

We've all grown up with stories of success that are straight lines—simple, clear narratives from A to B to Success. If you probe a little more deeply into someone's success story, however, you'll usually find that the straight-line story actually has a lot of angles, and that these multiple interests and angles are, in fact, critical to the person's success. In fact, it's been shown that traits common among successful people include their grasp on numerous, seemingly unrelated, topics, their facility with unusual areas of expertise, and their subsequent ability to improvise.

And in this economy, flexibility with multiple subjects and adaptability with new roles are proving still more important. A recent article in the *Harvard Business Review*, "How to Protect Your Job in a Recession," coauthored by Janet Banks, a former VP at Chase Manhattan Bank responsible for leadership development and succession planning, and Diane Coutu, a communications specialist at McKinsey & Company, maintains that this kind of fluidity is, in fact, critical for survival. Tight budgets demand managers who can wear multiple hats, find common interests with colleagues at every level of their organization, and move easily—and find parallels—among numerous, disparate subjects.

"Well, that's all well and good," you may be thinking, "but how can I prepare for demands I don't yet know exist?"

I recommend you adopt a Renaissance attitude.

What is the definition of this universal, or Renaissance, attitude? Well, Sir Kenneth Clark, host of the BBC television series *Civilisation: A Personal View*, said, "To live up to the Renaissance ideal of a universal man, one must touch life at many points." And according to Wikipedia, a Renaissance man is one who has developed "skills in all areas of knowledge, in physical development, in social accomplishments and in the arts."

Who's an example of a Renaissance man? Well, consider for a moment Leonardo da Vinci, whose breadth of expertise included art, architecture, mechanics, and anatomy, and among whose drawings, collected in codices and notebooks, are designs for both a tank and a submarine. These notebooks are so highly prized that Bill Gates (speaking of a Renaissance man—like his programs or hate them) paid $30 million for one.

Should you want a more modern example of someone whose ability to draw parallels across disparate areas of knowledge has led to tangible rewards, consider Dhani Jones, who, in addition to being an eight-year veteran of the NFL (where he's currently middle linebacker for the Cincinnati Bengals), has also parlayed his intelligence into a bowtie company and a television show on the Travel Channel, *Dhani Jones Tackles the Globe*, neither of which opportunities are likely to have come his way had he confined his interests solely to sports.

And let's not forget that—based on her ability to access both her maternal and professional sides—Michelle Obama's Secret Service code name is Renaissance.

So, how—in this day and age—to begin?

Most immediately, I would recommend changing the home page on your computer. If, for example, you've been thinking you needed more insight into world affairs, you could put up the BBC News home page (http://news.bbc.co.uk). If you've been wanting to do more reading but haven't had the time, consider changing it to the *Times Literary Supplement* (http://entertainment.timesonline .co.uk/tol/arts_and_entertainment/the_tls/); if you wish you knew more about the world of art, switch to the Metropolitan Museum (www.metmuseum.org). Once you're at the Met site, you can also subscribe to receive the "Artwork of the Day" feed). For a glimpse of the future, try http://www.arlingtoninstitute.org/; alternatively, http://www.wfs.org/ is an excellent way to open your mind to the fact that the world really will be different for you and your business when you wake up tomorrow.

If you've found that you need actual paper and ink in order to broaden your scope, you might try *Unmaking the West: "What-If?" Scenarios That Rewrite World History* (Tetlock, Lebow, and Parker, eds.). If you're seeking to strengthen your philosophical views, you could pick up contemporary philosopher Martin Cohen's *101 Philosophy Problems*, or if you simply want to fill some gaps in your education, you could make an investment in *The Intellectual Devotional* series.

Another inexpensive way to expand your mind is to steal a page from my high school English teacher. He said that good writing is *specific* writing ("Your characters should sit down under an elm or a maple, not just under a *tree*"), and he recommended for this reason that we all buy a visual dictionary. (Remember those? They provide detailed pictures of everyday objects and give you the exact names of each part of, say, a violin, your GI tract, or a jet.) I laughed at the time, but many years later I took his advice and bought DK Publishing's *Ultimate Visual Dictionary*, and now find it alternately fascinating and hilarious to browse. It's a very quick route to move from unconscious to conscious ignorance about any number of prosaic objects, and it *does* help your descriptive writing—not to mention save your skin when you're doing science homework with your kids. And by the way, getting one in a foreign language that you're learning will make you a star of the class. (Alternatively, you can also take my brother's approach—using Post-it notes to label every object in sight in your apartment in the language of your choice; but lest you think this is the path to fluency, NB: It only works for nouns!)

If you're willing to spend a bit more money, go back to college every time you commute or work out, via The Teaching Company (www.teach12.com), which offers hundreds of college courses by award-winning lecturers on a massive array of topics. Again, though—make sure that you're moving outside your comfort zone and choosing subjects about which you know almost nothing.

Robert Heinlein, commonly referred to as "the Dean of Science Fiction Writers," notes, "A human being should be able to change a diaper, plan an invasion, butcher a hog, conn a ship, design a building, write a sonnet, balance accounts, build a wall, set a bone, comfort the dying, take orders, give orders, cooperate, act alone, solve equations, analyze a new problem, pitch manure, program a computer, cook a tasty meal, fight efficiently, die gallantly. Specialization is for insects." And I assert that regardless of the manner in which you choose to begin taking in your new information, stretching your mind in this way will open your brain—and potentially your wallet—to previously unrecognized patterns, possibilities, and scenarios.

Corporate CliffsNotes

Every now and then, you find yourself in the position of needing to become an overnight expert on an area of an industry—or an entire industry—about which you know very little. Perhaps it's a call about a job outside your area of immediate expertise; perhaps it's needing to research the basics of an industry to which you are pitching. Whatever the reason, you need instant credibility, and you can feel instinctively that a glance at Wikipedia—or whatever else Google throws up—isn't going to cut it.

In these moments, I recommend you go immediately to http://harvardbusiness.org, home of Harvard Business School case studies. Covering disciplines from accounting to entrepreneurship, finance to marketing, negotiations to competitive strategy—and available for under ten dollars apiece—these bits of "potted knowledge" offer you the ability to speak with authority on subjects that you might otherwise have avoided. Designed to tell MBAs everything they need to know about the corporate drivers of a company or industry so they can offer intelligent analyses, these studies guarantee instant confidence.

7 | Recognize "Opportunity Costs"

It's no accident that the list of the six most influential words for a copywriter places "free" at number one: We are all drawn to the idea of getting something for nothing. (For the record, the remaining five—in order—are: "new," "amazing," "now," "how to," and "easy.") That said, when it comes to how you choose your projects—and how you spend your free time—I want you to begin asking yourself, "How free is free?"

Why? Because if you live to be seventy years old, you get 613,620 hours in your life—and that includes time spent sleeping.

This is not a big number.

I bring this up because one of the most valuable lessons I've learned over the years I've been in business comes from a client who mandated the following as a founding principle of her company: "Small projects take just as much (and maybe more) time and effort as big ones, so think big."

How did she come to this? Well, she and her husband currently have one of the largest, and most successful, real estate development firms in the world. But this certainly wasn't the case when they were starting out. When they began, they were scrambling—taking any and all jobs for fear that each opportunity would be their last, thinking, "Well, this isn't the greatest project, but how can we turn it down? We can do it with our eyes closed—it's free money!" The trouble with this attitude was that these smaller jobs were sucking away time and attention from their pitching the big projects—the reputation-making deals.

Now, I understand that in this economy it can be hard to wait for the big job. In these times, doing nothing is scarier than working toward the right thing. The trouble with this approach is that it has what economists call "an opportunity cost"—i.e., the time, effort, and money that you devote to that work is tied up and therefore can't be directed toward preparing for and pitching the big one.

Consider an example from the world of venture capitalists. For VCs, their (and your) most crucial constraint is *time*, as their work with lawyers, their analysis of the strengths and weaknesses of their management team, their conversations with customers and suppliers, etc.—the whole "due diligence" process—takes them just as long if they are investing $10 million in a potentially $200 million venture as it would if they were investing $1 million in a potentially $20 million venture. This is why they frequently set not only rigorous financial minimums on their investments, but why they frequently even set geographic constraints on them. For example, no matter how great the opportunity in, say, Houston, many will say, "Let's find some more great opportunities in Detroit, where we already have three other investments to watch."

The best of them ration time as carefully as they do money.

So as you consider what, when, and how to pursue the different leads that come your way, begin to ask yourself, "Is now the time for this? Is my energy better spent elsewhere? If I decide to do this, how much time am I willing to spend?" And, finally and most important, "If it seems I have no other options, what can I do simultaneously to keep myself on track with regard to my real goals?"

Why is that last consideration most important? Because I want you to begin making the distinction between being powerless and being helpless. Yes, you might currently be in a position where you have to take jobs that don't appear to be contributing to making your dreams come true, but this doesn't mean that you can't continue to put aside some time, even if it's only fifteen minutes a day—one networking phone call, one pitch letter sent to a potential client, one résumé sent out to pursue "the big one."

I'm afraid I feel the same with regard to how free time is spent.

I'm not saying it isn't important to have time to recharge, to blow off steam, to be off duty—whatever you want to call it. But that time needs to be as carefully considered as your work time, and I find that's rarely the case. While most of us know exactly how many hours we worked last week, very few of us can give an exact count of how many hours we spent—and here's one of the most overused words in advertising, *for a reason*—relaxing.

FYI: For advertisers, "relaxing" is code for separating you from your cash.

Please note: I am not characterizing learning a new skill set, or honing an existing one, as wasting time. If you're a music enthusiast and you decide to spend some time learning to play the guitar, or you're an amateur gardener and you take a few hours to go through seed catalogs, that's time well spent. What I'm talking about is time spent drooped on the sofa watching *reruns* of reality shows, or surfing the Web in pursuit of the newest video in which a dog has been taught to play the piano.

If you think I'm being too strict, consider the idea that in the same way the quality of the food you put in your body affects your ability to perform at your best—which is why you want to make the cleanest, most nutritious choices available—the quality of the books you read, movies you see, people you spend time with, activities you pursue, etc., also affects your ability to perform at your best. If you're putting junk in your mind, it's unlikely it will have the stamina to pursue your passions. We're a nation that loves a diet, a purge, or a cleanse: Put yourself on a mental fast-food fast.

How to begin? I would recommend starting by simply noticing what you're doing with your time—watching television, surfing the Web, hanging out with friends—and make a note of approximately how many hours a week it's consuming.

I would then have you ask yourself, "Is this time spent contributing to my dreams, or just daydreaming? Is this person someone who motivates and stimulates me to be my best, or is this someone whose only appeal is to my reptilian brain?"

In short, what is the opportunity cost of this decision? Given the finite number of hours available, is this someone or something I want to spend my time with or on?

I'm not saying your answer won't be "Yes! Yes, thanks, Frances, I don't need to be an overachiever every hour of every day of my life." Or, "Guess what, Frances? Today is, in fact, the day I set aside to put my brain in neutral and get caught up on exactly what's been keeping *American Idol* afloat all these years." Or, "You know what, Frances? You can take a number, because I've set today aside to watch Formula One racing with my kid with the volume up so high our ears bleed."

For the record, I'm fine with all these answers. Why? Because they indicate you've made a choice. Everybody needs a "cheat day" in their diet, and everybody needs dropout time in their life.

But in the same way consistent exercise resets your basal metabolic rate, the effect of consistently healthy mental choices resets your mental metabolic rate, so I won't be surprised if, after a day of sprawl and gorge, your brain doesn't start feeling like you're packing on "brain flab"—flab that will begin melting away moments after you stand up, lace up your mental sneakers, and begin taking concrete steps to create the career, and the life, you want and deserve.

The Chute You Pack May Be Your Own

In the Marines, "riggers"—the people who pack (i.e., reassemble after use) parachutes for other Marines—have to make at least one jump a month. Who packs their 'chute? They do: One of the parachutes that *they* packed for others to use is chosen at random, and the rigger has to "jump it." This system helps make sure that no one gets sloppy—after all, "The chute you're packing may be your own."

The Roman army used a similar technique to make sure bridges and

aqueducts were safe: The person who designed the arches had to stand
under each arch while the scaffolding was being removed.

If you want your company to last as long as Roman bridges have,
ask yourself if everyone is *truly* responsible for outcomes by these
measures—and if you yourself are. Are you performing every task with
the concentration and commitment that you might if a life depended
on it?

8 | See the Whole Board; Think Several Moves Deep

Garry Kasparov, the greatest chess player in the history of the world, and now a dissident Russian politician, claims there are only two keys to playing great chess: See the whole board and think several moves deep. (Warren Buffett, by the way, agrees, saying that *the* key question in economics is "And then what?")

How can you apply this idea to a business environment? (After all, the first four moves in chess offer 318,979,584,000 possible opening games, and life offers even more.) By taking an expansive view of your business mandate and your customer's experience. How can you do this? By looking at your core business processes not as a single snapshot or diagram in a conference room, but as a *flow:*

- Consider how you develop products and services

- Look at how you generate demand for these

- Analyze how you fulfill that demand

My goal is to have you begin to see this chain as an integrated, living process whose aim is maximum customer satisfaction and value, start to finish.

One of the best examples of this concept I know comes from Virgin Atlantic Airlines, a company universally acknowledged to have changed the way we fly. One of the ways they did this was by considering what the flying experience was like *outside* the airplane: What could they do to improve the way people felt about both their trip to the airport and their time *in* the airport? Some of the ideas they implemented include offering passengers a limousine service to pick them up at their home and drive them to their terminal. Another was to institute more luxurious lounges, and to make them available to premium fliers, both coming and going. (After all, one needs a shower a lot more on arrival than before takeoff!) They also, of course, treated their premium passengers like adults in flight, offering them the "luxury" of simply raiding a picnic basket to get their own snacks. Their ability to consider the entire travel experience—not just the portion they were technically responsible for—is one of the reasons they've led their field.

With this in mind, then, how can you step back from your immediate situation—take a more global perspective? For example, if you own a business, have you considered offering free or discount parking to your customers? Working with your chamber of commerce to improve the lighting in the parking lot? Speaking with the businesses around you about adding trees, window boxes, or shrubbery to make the surroundings more compelling? This is in effect what New York's Times Square Partnership and other neighborhood associations have done. They have hired their own street-cleaning crews and security guards, because they realize that people's shopping experiences don't start at their stores' front doors, but at the *customers'* front doors (or at least, well before their individual shops). They view a purchase as a process and a relationship. In short, just as the best way to see if your houseguests will have a nice experience is to sleep for one night in your guest room, one recipe for success in business is to truly "walk a mile" in your customers' shoes.

Admittedly, it's hard to think big picture at times when things are tight—or to consider spending money on seeming nonessentials. That said, it's at times like these that customers make choices based on the smallest of variables. Providing customers with a "complete experience" was certainly how coffee shops ended up in bookstores, and why Starbucks is now the largest public wi-fi provider in America; and I'm positive it's why my muffler shop has added both a television and a table of the latest magazines to its waiting area, and why my gym has soap, shampoo, lotion, and hair dryers in the changing rooms.

What are some questions you might ask yourself, or some tools you can use to elicit this information?

- Consider not only how the competition is doing business, but also how your favorite businesses are engaging you. Are there elements of their customer experience that you can tweak to improve your own?

- Organize a focus group with your best customers. In exchange for X amount of free product or service, ask them how or what they might improve about your business or service. You can create your own focus group at sites like www.zoomerang.com or www.surveymonkey.com.

- Include a "suggestions for improvement" section on your website. (This should include an automatic reply thanking them for their input. If their suggestion is implemented, I would further follow up with a note letting them know that, too. It's a fantastic, easy way to help your customers get invested in your success while improving your business—the ultimate win/win.)

As you can see, no matter the size of your business, considering the entire flow of your customers' experience is likely to end with you saying "Checkmate" to your competition.

Who's Your "Fish"?

When you're headed into a sales situation, it's important to take a step back and ask "Who's the 'fish' here?"

What does that mean? As Warren Buffett's business partner, Charlie Munger, relates, "Many years ago, a Pasadena friend of mine made fishing tackle. I looked at this fishing tackle—it was green and purple and blue; I'd never seen anything like them. I asked him, 'God! Do fish bite these lures?' He said to me, 'Charlie, I don't sell to fish.' "

His point? Fish will eat just about anything, but we're unlikely to buy just about anything.

Pet toy companies and supermarkets are working the same angle when they position Fido's potential new toys low in the aisle—because let's face it, those bright colors and cute bone shapes don't offer Fido any more fun. They do, however, appeal to your child, who is often the driver behind this type of sale.

Life insurance firms are also unlikely "fishing companies," but, in fact, they are keeping two fish in mind. Who are their fish? What they discovered is that among married couples, women tend to prompt men to buy more insurance. But it tends to be men who actually choose the insurance company and policy. With this in mind, companies have geared different parts of the insurance sales cycle to this pattern and employ different kinds of "bait" in those moments. The advertisements for insurance aimed mostly at women with children are built around emotions (i.e., love and fear). These tend to show a family playing on the beach (in the mist) and ask in soft tones, "How would your loved ones cope if something happened to you? Take care of those you treasure with our term life policies starting at just . . ." These get the moms revved up. But since the moms don't tend to run out and buy the policies—they ask the dads to do so after watching those ads—different bait is needed for them. The ads for the dads, then, stress either value or financial stability: "We've been helping families secure their financial futures for over seventy years," or "*Consumer Reports* consistently ranks our policies . . ." They also take the hassle-free approach: "No physical required . . .," etc.

Of course, these are gender stereotypes, but the point is that these companies don't mix lures—they don't do the misty family pictures and then talk about their customer satisfaction ratings in the same advertisements.

The proof is in the exception: The only time you do see mixed bait in the insurance industry is for a different fish entirely—senior citizens. If you open retiree magazines, you'll see that they are sold life insurance with ads like: "For only pennies a day, and without any physical exam required, you can spare those you love the worry of . . ." When there's a single decision-maker, the insurance companies use hybrid bait.

So, before you go into a sales situation (which, one way or another, is any situation), always be clear about who is the driver, gatekeeper, or facilitator of the sale and who is the potential end user, and make sure you have "bait" for both.

9 | Pick Limiting Features

There are few things more debilitating than standing up in a meeting—all attention on you—and presenting your big idea only to have someone ask, "Well, what if X happens?" and having that be the moment you realize you haven't actually given X any thought.

Conversely, there are few things as satisfying as presenting your idea in a meeting—all attention on you—seeing your archenemy open his or her mouth to ask the X question and being able to say, "In the event of X, we've already considered the following options."

Gotcha.

In my world this is known as "picking limiting features." And while we all know the value of articulating limiting features when giving directions to others—for example, telling your weekend guests, "If you pass the white church you've gone too far," thus ensuring that as they drive toward your house they make a point of keeping their eyes open for any and all white churches—few of us make a practice of thinking through mental limiting features: i.e., thinking ahead of time about what facts would make us reverse course or alter our plan. What I've discovered is that if you always review a plan employing the metaphor of a journey, consistently considering what factors or incidents might make you change or reverse your course, you'll increase your odds of success; and that if you don't do this, you don't really have a plan or a theory as much as a wish or a hope.

For example, perhaps you've been planning the launch of a new line of organic frozen veggie burgers. The tricky thing is that you've heard rumors that your competitor has plans to launch a rival—and near-identical—product four months before yours is scheduled to appear. Knowing this is a possibility means that you might not only mention those rumors in your presentation, but you also say, "Because we hear X company has a similar product in play, we are exploring nontraditional selling outlets for our product: nursing homes and hospitals that are looking for meat alternatives. If we get a strong response, our plan is to change our packaging to declare this the new 'Gray/Green' line of burgers, as this is something we know X hasn't contemplated." This is an example of preemptive planning that's guaranteed to leave your listeners impressed.

One way many companies identify limiting features in order to enhance their packaging or product offerings, is by running focus groups in which targeted questions elicit what customers like best about their product and what features they're indifferent to. For example, if you run a vitamin company that's considering expanding into kids' vitamins, but you've been getting pushback from shareholders about the budget, you can put together a focus group of your existing customers, whose feedback might allow you to say, "What we've discovered is that our customers are adamant about having a childproof safety cap on our kids' vitamin package, and they don't want us to use high-fructose corn syrup. They are less concerned with making sure the vitamins come in kid-friendly shapes and colors. Consequently, if we have to make some decisions about where to spend, we're going to put the extra cash into making sure our packaging meets their safety concerns and our ingredients are of the highest quality."

Making a practice of exploring and articulating limiting features is especially useful when you're leading a team, because outlining the telltale signs necessitating a course change means that other people can watch for them as well and will be less inclined to panic should you have to change your plans mid-launch. In fact, they may even end up taking pleasure in the opportunity to exhibit their versatility.

For example, one day a client called to say she and her husband, who had launched a new wine bar–cum–coffee shop a few months earlier with a laudable "Nothing's going to stop us" attitude, had bumped into a limiting feature they'd articulated in their planning: A big part of their launch PR had been built around offering "flights" of wine, and an existing establishment had just begun such flights, with great fanfare. Because my clients had talked through this possibility with their team, a staff member had not only made a note of it when she saw it on their competitor's menu, but she'd walked into the next team meeting having already thought through what my clients' company might do instead, which was to offer flights of cheese, or coffee. The consequence of this was that instead of having an "Oh no!" head-holding, brow-mopping conversation, everyone got very fired up about how they could do it better.

So, while it's not necessary to have a full-blown plan for every contingency, adopting this mental discipline, and leading a team with this approach, reminds everyone there is a lot you, and they, can do to manage — and potentially profit from — life's changing events.

"If I Only Had X Back at My Office . . ."

One of the many limiting features I have my clients think through when we're working on a presentation is what they'll do when—not if—their technology goes down. With that in mind, we write their deck, and practice, so that the presentation is effective without technology *before* we factor in what visuals they might include.

Another limiting feature I ask them to consider is what they'll do when they arrive at their destination and, for whatever reason, they no longer have the document or presentation they need. Here are three techniques I've given them to help prevent disaster:

1. Phone a friend: Before you travel, send emails to close colleagues or family that say, "Can you please keep the attached safe for me?" Your bags can get lost, your computer can get stolen, your plans can change, your own email system (to which I frequently send

things for backup) can go down. If you can reach one of those friends on the phone, he or she will have the presentation or document you need. It's free peace of mind.

2. Slightly more high-tech and secure is "GoToMyPC" (www .gotomypc.com). If you have confidential documents that you can't email to friends, I recommend this service: It lets you log in to your home machine and hard drive from any browser in the world. Call your spouse/partner, ask them to turn on your home PC and modem, and soon you'll be getting that file you wanted.

3. If you have a home office, I recommend that you buy a label maker and use it to label all your files: Keeping this discipline up means that in a pinch, you can call someone and ask them to look in your filing cabinets to find something for you. They won't know the system as well as you, but at least they're not confronted with the added problem of deciphering your handwriting to find the crucial report that you need express-mailed to you.

10 | "No One Can Make You Feel Inferior Without Your Consent"

I This quote from Eleanor Roosevelt is particularly helpful to consider as many of us find ourselves posting our résumés yet again, because—despite the pervasive impact of today's "retracting" economy—it can be easy to think it's somehow your fault that you've reentered the job market, to beat yourself up thinking, "If only I had done X," or "If only I hadn't said Y." As one of my clients said, "It doesn't help to know other people are going through it. When it happened to me, it felt personal—it felt like *I* failed."

The trouble with this is that this sense of personal failure has the potential to influence the way you begin to think about your former situation, making it still more difficult to talk about how and why you were let go. With this in mind, then, let's look at some language you can use to ensure you end up on offense instead of defense.

The Foul-Weather Friend Response:

You've all heard the term "fair-weather friend," which describes a person who's always around so long as the sun is shining and the seas are calm. Unfortunately, foul-weather friends also exist—people who miraculously show up in your life the day your divorce papers are delivered, when you find yourself in the emergency room, or during the planning of your parent's funeral, but are somehow never free to come to your holiday party, your child's graduation, or your anniversary celebration. These psychic vampires generally open with "What happened?" instead of "What can I do?" as their ultimate goal is not your well-being but instead detail-collecting, in an effort to make themselves feel better about what's going on in their lives and to get a boost of self-importance from being "there for you." You will also find they have time to spread your story far and wide.

For this particular category I recommend keeping your explanation short and sweet. "Well, I closed the shop." Or, "Well, I got laid off." *That's it.* Further detail is unnecessary. Should they follow up with "Oh, I'm so sorry. Did you see it coming?" all you need to say is "Thank you. Yes. (Or no.) I appreciate your concern." They are not entitled to more.

The Potential Employer Response:

Obviously, things become somewhat more complex when a potential employer asks about the reason behind your changed status. That said, I continue to recommend keeping the particulars of your situation to a minimum, and instead making a broader statement about the state of your industry: "Yes, a number of people in my area were also let go due to downsizing. As you know, my sector was hit hard due to X, Y, and Z"; or, "Yes, an inability to raise our third round of funding necessitated some cuts all around. As you know, venture capital is thin on the ground in this economy." Then use that as a springboard for talking about what you learned from the experience, and how you plan to apply that knowledge to your new position. "What I've discovered is that tackling challenges outside my comfort zone actually inspires me—I like a sharp learning curve. This is one of the primary reasons I came in to talk to you. I very much admire the diversified, hands-on approach you ask of your employees." Or, "What I learned is the value of a good fund-raiser, so that's where I've put my energy in the intervening months"—very few people look bored when you mention you know how to raise money. "With regard to how I might raise money for you, I was thinking of X, Y, and Z."

The World of Commerce Response:

When you're talking with your world of commerce—your credit card company, your kid's school, your doctor, anyone to whom you currently owe money—you will again want to stay out of the details or your feelings about what has occurred. Instead just state the facts and your immediate plan of action: This is how much I owe you; this is my plan for getting the money to you. The critical piece here is to take the initiative. Yes, these can be gruesome calls to make, but ducking them is not going to make their resolution any easier. All that will achieve is to make you feel still worse about yourself, and my hunch is you've had a bellyful of that. In fact, my guess is that making these calls will leave you feeling better because, as George Bernard Shaw said, "No man who is occupied in doing a very difficult thing, and doing it very well, ever loses his self-respect." Additionally, you may be pleasantly surprised to discover, as one of my clients did, that this isn't the first call of this kind the person at the other end of the phone has gotten and that, in fact, she or he has put together a number of payment plan options for those in your situation.

The Family Response:

One of the most critical elements to consider is how to talk with your family about what's happened. With relatives, it's again important to weed out the foul-weather types from those who genuinely have your best interests at heart. When talking with your kids, my recommendation would be to put the facts to them simply and without too much detail: This is what's occurred, this is the plan we have put together for handling it, this is how I'm going to be needing your help. I would also make a point of stressing all the things you still do have: health, each other, your collective intelligence and creativity, etc. While you may seem too "team spirit-y," I'm guessing your kids are going to surprise you with their willingness to help—another aspect of wealth it's important to acknowledge and cherish.

What Two Things . . .

At my house this sentence ends, "do not improve the situation?" The answers? Panic and self-pity. (The last time I was feeling sorry for myself, I was told to Google the poem "Invictus" by William Ernest Henley—and read it with the knowledge that Henley wrote it the day after his left leg was amputated.) Too often, however, we default to these emotions when we feel overwhelmed.

The trouble with this is not that these emotions arise. It's normal—it's human—for them to come up. The trouble begins when we indulge them. As Benjamin Disraeli said, "Grief is the agony of an instant, the indulgence of grief the blunder of a life." (Or as Al-Anon—somewhat less elegantly, but no less succinctly—puts it, "There are no victims, only volunteers.")

What, then, am I asking you to do? I'm asking you to make a habit of mentally stepping back from these thoughts, breathing, and doing nothing for a moment—just a moment. Because if you can begin to recognize when you've fallen into these patterns, you will automatically begin to recalibrate.

Breakups Are Like Handguns

This line is one my brother offered me as I exited a cataclysmic romance—his point, of course, being that momentous decisions are almost always improved by a twenty-four-hour waiting period.

In these days of hair-trigger tension—and constantly shifting relationships—this is particularly important to remember. Because while it may feel good to use your exit interview as an opportunity to say all the things you've bottled up over the years, or to take the time while you're cleaning out your office to do a few quick character assassinations of those in charge, the possibility that you will be working with many of these people again in various future incarnations is very real.

Far better, then, to step away from the situation, say everything you're longing to say to a trusted, uninvolved third party, and walk out with your head held high: an elegant choice that ensures the rumor mill will be filled with stories of your poise, not your bitterness, and guarantees that when you run into your former bosses and colleagues in the upcoming weeks, months, and years, you're able to greet them from a position of strength.

11 | Don't Break Your Own Heart

Swami Kripalvananda said, "My beloved child, break your heart no longer. Each time you judge yourself you break your own heart." This section ends with this quote, and this essay, because I think that in times like these it's easy to get caught up in thinking how you could, or should, have done things differently. But if the way we talk to ourselves *about* ourselves is shaming, blaming, angry, destructive—pejorative in any way—how can we expect to show up in the world confident in our ability to contribute?

From what I've observed, the trouble often begins when we begin comparing our insides to other people's outsides, a nasty mental cul-de-sac that can lead to an internal dialogue along the lines of "I can't believe I let that happen" or "I'm such an idiot" or "How could I have been so blind?"

For example, I have one client who'd worked with a public relations firm for the last ten years. For the two years before the firm declared Chapter 11, he had been hearing rumors of cost-cutting on the employee level combined with the acquisition of still larger and more lavish houses and cars by the CEO. My client's trouble was that not only did he like the guy at the top—the CEO had taken a chance on him when no one else would—he was also scared to move, as he had a mortgage, credit card bills, school fees for his kids. . . . So he stayed. And when the firm did indeed go belly-up, the death throes were compounded by my client's anger at himself for not having left when he could. His brain became a nonstop feedback loop of self-loathing—which only added to his stress at having to look for a new job.

At this point, the request I made of him, and I would make of you, is to step back and ask yourself: Would I speak to a close friend that way? My guess is you wouldn't. Or, as my friend Bill said to his girlfriend, Sarah, when she was running herself down, "Hey, don't talk about my girlfriend like that."

The tricky part is that, as the saying goes, familiarity breeds contempt. We're often so deep inside our own story, and consequently so conscious of all our mistakes, that we forget to give ourselves credit for all the kind, smart, or strategic things we do, instead choosing to focus on all the things we think we could or should be doing differently.

My point is that you do have a choice, and the more productive choice to make is to shift your focus from self-improvement to self-acceptance. I'm not saying it's easy, but I am saying it's possible.

This is not to say you get a bye on creative procrastination, heedless decisions, or generally poor behavior—these are never acceptable, and if you notice a pattern to their occurrence it needs to be addressed. What I am saying is that most of us are doing the best we can with the tools that we've got, and cutting ourselves some slack is going to get us farther than beating ourselves up. Your willingness to think the best of yourself is going to help others think the best of you, and increasing your awareness of the story you tell yourself is the quickest way to have that story change.

We all deserve a great story.

With this in mind, I offer you the following:

When I first started my company (and please note that this was career change number five) one of my advisers took me out to lunch and said, "Here's what nobody tells you: There's plenty of room at the top—so come on up."

That knocked me out. In a world where many successful people like to shroud their decision-making in mystery—preferring instead to make their good fortune seem inevitable to them and unattainable by you—finding someone willing to say, "Hey, when you're ready, there's more than enough to go around" was indescribably heartening.

And I promise that when you believe this to be true, know on a cellular level that it is your right to be at the top, you will be.

Business Class Is About More Than the Salted Almonds

Some partnerships are tight with money for junior employees. In one respect, at least, one of the most successful partnerships on earth is not: McKinsey & Company has all their consultants, no matter how junior, fly business class. Why? They reason that every once in a while one of their consultants will get into a conversation with a fellow business-class passenger, and that fellow passenger will end up a customer of McKinsey's services. If you travel a lot, and your employer doesn't do this (or if, like me, you're self-employed and usually not willing to shell out for business class), there's still a way to pursue this strategy, or at least a variation of it: "Priority Pass" (www .prioritypass.com). Priority Pass is a service that for a reasonable annual fee lets you use business-class lounges at over six hundred airports around the world. While you'll still be flying coach, you'll be rubbing elbows with business-class people while you wait. In addition, you'll stress less about layovers, arrive more relaxed, and probably make a good contact the next time you're stuck in Denver.

Summing It Up:

- Circumnavigating, removing, or changing your attitude is far more manageable (and likely) if you break it down into discrete steps—and even small changes begin to rewire your brain. Improving one skill every month means that in a year you will have twelve new habits.

- Sometimes opportunity looks like hard work: Don't shirk. As Samuel Goldwyn said, "I find that the harder I work, the more luck I seem to have."

- Actively create camaraderie in meetings by picking small-talk topics ahead of time, eating and drinking what you're offered, writing down what people tell you, making notes immediately upon leaving for use in follow-up documents, and ensuring you loop your team in on all communication information.

- Despite the power of the World Wide Web, business cards aren't going out of fashion anytime soon. Given this—and the fact that people prefer different modes of communication—make sure you have cards, and that those cards offer multiple channels for reaching you, including your landline, mobile number, Skype number, and email and snail mail addresses.

- If you're presenting a chaotic, dirty shop front to the world, it's hard for those around you to believe in the quality of the work you can, or will, produce. The phrase "Look good, feel good" can, and should, be applied to your office as well as your person.

- One common denominator among successful people is their grasp on seemingly unrelated topics. With this in mind, adopt a Renaissance attitude: Challenge yourself to learn outside your area of expertise.

- The same way the quality of the food you eat affects your body's performance, the quality of the work you choose, and how you spend your free time, affects your mind's performance. Give your brain the mental nutrition it needs to perform at its peak.

- Take an expansive view of your business mandate and your customer's experience. Maximizing the potential of every step in the chain will ensure your customer's satisfaction from start to finish.

- Picking mental "limiting features" dramatically increases the odds of your success, as we are more likely to notice an event if we've anticipated its possibility, and changing course is far easier if its likelihood has always been part of the conversation.

- Many people will have an opinion about the choices you've made, and are making, in your life. At the end of the day, however, only one person's opinion of you matters: your own.

- Increasing your awareness of the story you tell yourself is the quickest way to have that story change. You "break your own heart" when that story is blaming, shaming—pejorative in any way. You need to tell yourself—and believe—there's plenty of room for you at the top.

SECTION TWO
KNOW

The well-known philosopher J. Krishnamurti said, "To know is to be ignorant. Not to know is the beginning of wisdom," and it's certainly true that assuming a "beginner's mind" is critical to gaining new perspectives on people and situations with which you are or aren't familiar—you simply can't learn what you think you already know.

That said, we also live in a world where knowledge is power—and where ignorance of certain kinds of information can prove a severe handicap. Additionally, there are those small, seemingly insignificant kinds of information that we all wonder about but haven't had the time to research, that nevertheless take up an inordinate amount of our mental space when we trip over them in conversation or social situations, making it difficult for us to keep our attention on the big picture.

Section Two, then, offers the practical information critical to surviving in today's business environment, everything from how to get your résumé to the top of the pile, to how to outprepare your interviewer, to how to shine when you're in the hot seat. The necessary criteria for expressing yourself clearly, accurately, and elegantly in every scenario—in person, on the telephone, or via text, email, or snail mail—will be explored, as will the values of play, timing, and silence. The "soft answer that turneth away wrath" will be considered, as will a means of interpreting others' verbal dodges. Possible answers to numerous frequently asked questions will be considered, as will the art of interrupting someone whose answer has, perhaps, gone on too long.

While there may be moments in this section where you think, "I already know *that*," I'm also hoping there will be moments when you think, "I always wondered about that," or "Is that why other people do/say that?" or "Okay, I didn't realize I need to know that," and are happy you have the answer in hand, leaving your mind free to answer the hard question, tackle the tricky team meeting, and source the creativity and flexibility necessary to succeed in any high-stakes environment.

12 | Manners Matter

These days interviews and sales calls take all kinds of forms, among them business lunches and dinners. Generally the final round in a series of hurdles you've had to clear, they are less about assessing your business acumen—this has been solid enough to get you to the final round—than about seeing how you are able to interact with others in collegial and social situations. In short, this is where the smallest of small details is what separates those who receive an offer from those who receive a phone call saying, "I'm so sorry to have to tell you this—it was a really tough decision—but we've decided to go with someone else."

How to Wow covered the broad strokes of socializing with others: Be on time, order food that's easy to manage, follow your host's lead with regard to beginning with small talk vs. diving into a business conversation; don't drink, don't discuss your dietary habits, don't say you've got to "hit the head." Since covering those basics, I've realized there are many more pitfalls than I was aware of. Here's an example I heard from one of my clients. (Yes, it's true.)

As you know, multiple rounds of interviews are common in the financial industry. In this instance, the gentleman in question had met with a number of firm members, and for this meeting, his third, he'd been invited to have lunch at the local Chinese restaurant with the guys who'd make up his team. With everyone seated, an order was put in for a number of dishes that could be shared. Food began arriving and this gentleman—perhaps confusing his Chinese restaurant etiquette with his Japanese restaurant etiquette—reached into the basket of moo shoo pancakes, plucked one out, and used it as a face towel.

It seems he didn't get the job.

While this may seem an extreme example, there are numerous ways—large and small—of knocking yourself out of the running for your dream job. Since I would hate to have any etiquette misstep undermine your hard work, here's a down-and-dirty list of things to know before your next meeting or lunch:

1. It seems insane that I have to put this in writing, but experience has proven I must. Wash your hair. Clean your nails. Do not chew gum. (Altoids are great to ensure fresh breath before you arrive, but they need to be gone before you go through the door.) If you shave, shave properly, and that morning.

2. That cleanliness advisory given, I wouldn't recommend turning up smelling so strongly of scent that it lingers after you do.

3. Please do not wear your sunglasses, either on your face or on your head. Unless you're talking through the deal points of your new record contract at the Urth Caffé on Melrose (or you're a professional poker player), you look foolish.

4. Do not have MP3 player headphones hanging out or visible (much less in your ears). The same goes for wireless earpieces for your cellphone—take them off and put them away.

5. If you carry a briefcase, make sure that it isn't overstuffed and chaotic-looking: Remove all candy wrappers, old sandwiches, etc.

6. While I have no objection to the flaunting of chest hair or cleavage on your own time, it needs to stay under wraps in a business setting. I would also recommend covering any tattoos you might have, at least until you get a sense of the environment or culture you may be entering. The same goes for ankle bracelets and visible body piercings.

7. When arriving at or leaving the building, remember that you don't know who's on the elevator with you—or who might get on. Don't be the guy with the phone against his head yakking about what's just about to—or what just did—happen.

8. The same is true when you're in the ladies' or men's room. Again, as bizarre as it may seem that I have to write this down, office and restaurant bathrooms are not extensions of your home bathroom. This is not the time to make personal calls, do a complete makeup or wardrobe overhaul, or settle in with a magazine or book.

9. Political buttons, religious pins, *Star Trek* badges, etc., have their place, but not in interviews or on business occasions. No matter how committed you may be to a cause, these topics are potential minefields; best to keep your affiliation decorations for personal occasions.

10. Should you need to blow your nose during the meeting or lunch, please excuse yourself to do so. If a sneeze catches you unawares—and unprepared with a handkerchief—please excuse yourself to wash your hands.

11. If they take you to a restaurant, you can be pretty sure that they're checking your table manners: Now is not the time to order dishes that you adore but that are hard to eat neatly. (Save spareribs and lobster for your celebratory lunch after you get the job.) In the same vein, don't be too picky or fussy when presented with the menu—your primary objective is to make a good impression on your future employers, not show them that you are a gourmand (unless, of course, the job involves food).

12. Aside from the fact that my mother always impressed on me that salting your food before tasting it was an insult to the chef, I've heard that those in the business world view it as indicative of

poor impulse control—see it as an indication you may make judgments without having all the facts.

13. Don't drink, even if they do.

14. Nobody—and I repeat, nobody—is so important they need to check their PDA during a meeting or lunch. The people with whom you're talking need to have 100 percent of your focus. If you can't give them this when you're sitting in front of them, why would they believe you can give them this when you aren't?

15. I would also request that you refrain from looking at your PDA in between standing up from your table in the restaurant and exiting the door, or until you've left the building in which your meeting took place. You need to give your goodbyes the same attention you did your hellos.

16. If you are with team members, again, do not discuss your meeting in the elevator. I would also not recommend debriefing it within a two-block radius of the building or in any nearby restaurant. You don't know who's listening.

Alternatively, there are a number of things you can do that will contribute to your confidence, reassure others, or just flat knock me out with their fabulousness. Following are a few of those:

1. Should you have to ring a doorbell or buzzer that someone answers (as opposed to "buzzing" you in), take one step back from the door after pressing the button for entry: You'll look better to the person answering the door at that distance.

2. As you know, when you step in from being out in the cold, it's almost always necessary to blow your nose. Knowing this, step into a nearby store, or arrive at the venue a few minutes early, and take care of this—repeated sniffing as you're being introduced is as hard on you as it is on those around you. *How*

to Wow offered the rule of thumb "Two is one, and one is none": this is never more true than for handkerchiefs/Kleenex.

3. Conversely, if it is hot, leave extra time to get there so you're not rushed, and carry a handkerchief to clean up (i.e., mop your brow) before going in.

4. If you wear glasses, clean them thoroughly before going in. It helps you see, but it also helps others see your eyes, which builds trust. (I know of one man who was offered a cloth to clean his glasses halfway through an interview because the interviewer found them so distractingly smudged.)

5. Despite what you may have been told, chivalry's not dead. In fact, it's welcome wherever this wow expert goes. One of my most elegant male friends collects all the coat check stubs from his lunch partners, retrieves their belongings, and has small bills at the ready to tip the attendant.

While many of you are likely to have had the majority of this information at your fingertips, I'm hoping there were one or two things that were new to you—or that, at the very least, made you laugh. On that note, one of the greatest compliments you can offer your interviewer, meeting attendees, or lunch partners is your enthusiasm. Bearing the above in mind—and coupling it with genuine enthusiasm for becoming a part of the group—is sure to net you the offer or deal you are looking for.

Elevator Etiquette

As I'm sure you know, a ninety-second elevator commute can be an eternity if your compatriots neglect certain basics of elevator etiquette. Here are a few things I'd prefer not to hear or see again:

1. Although it's lovely that you want to get upstairs and start working, please wait to make sure everyone's exited the elevator before attempting to get on.
2. If you're just about to miss one, please don't stick a hand or foot in the path of the electronic eye. I guarantee another's coming, and those already on board are just as anxious to get upstairs as you are.
3. If you are riding with one other person, take their cue with regard to commenting on the weather, etc. Some people prefer to be alone with their thoughts. (That said, if you are riding with your CEO, VP, or immediate colleague, please do acknowledge that by saying, "Good morning/afternoon.")
4. Saying "Excuse me" when you need to exit a crowded elevator is a lovely idea. Saying "Excuse me" before the doors have opened raises everybody's hackles.
5. For reasons I've failed to fathom, many coworkers choose to continue private conversations in these small spaces. Trust me, no one else wants, or needs, to know the details of your commute, your dental appointment, or your one-night stand.
6. Similarly, the elevator is not an extension of your office. Wrap up phone calls before boarding. Don't take them once you're on.
7. Please do not feel compelled to say "It looks like we're on the local" should you be stopping on every floor.
8. If you are alone on the elevator, please don't assume you are unwatched. Unless you want to provide security with some laughs, this is not the time for a major wardrobe or nasal adjustment.

Off-Duty Do's and Don'ts

In addition to meeting for lunch, job candidates are often asked to attend social events, or to play sports, as part of the screening process. With this in mind, here are a few do's and don'ts for attending the theater, symphony, or opera, meeting at someone's private club, or playing tennis or golf:

At the Theater, Opera, Symphony:

- Ask what others are wearing. If they are going to be in suits and ties/dresses, you need to be as well.
- A note on vocabulary: You go to *hear,* not to *see,* an opera.
- Punctuality is *vital.* You will simply not be let in if you are five minutes late.
- When taking a seat in the center of an aisle, you always pass other people in that row facing them, not putting your backside in their face. If you are being passed, stand up if at all possible.
- Blinking lights mean you should get to your seat (AND turn off your phone).
- Don't overdo scent.
- Don't talk during a performance. No, really: Don't talk. Again: Is your phone ringer off?
- Don't eat, drink, chew gum, etc.—you can eat and drink during intermission. Simply don't chew gum. If you can place drink orders before intermission, do.
- Avoid jingling jewelry and large hairstyles.
- Knowing when to clap can be tricky—technically, you should only do so at the end of a scene or act. Watch others for clues.
- Do not try to sneak out before the curtain calls: It is rude to the audience, and especially rude to the performers, who have just given their all for you. This applies to encores, too.

At City and Country Clubs:

- Check the dress code—it is likely to be quite "old-fashioned." You can do this by consulting your host or calling the club.
- As you enter, tell a member of the door staff your name and whom you are meeting. He will tell you where you can wait if your host is not there yet, and where to find your host if he or she arrived before you.

- If you do arrive before your host, stay in the waiting room to which you are directed. Other than going to the restroom, do not be tempted to wander or "look around."
- Never bring out business papers or work of any sort. If your host does not raise business topics in conversation, you shouldn't either.
- In general, speak 20 percent more softly than you are used to.
- Almost all clubs restrict use of cellphones—let your host be your guide, but plan on being out of contact electronically entirely while you are in the clubhouse.
- Never offer to pay, and do not try to tip staff.
- If using the club's athletic facilities, make sure your shoes are clean before entering, and be scrupulous about not hogging equipment, wiping down equipment after use, and putting things back where you found them. Avoid Neanderthal displays of grunting, "hydrating," etc. Do not be irritatingly competitive. Women should wear sports bras; men, jockstraps.
- Always communicate with club staff through your host, not directly (e.g., your host asks waiters and waitresses to get refills for you— you don't order them from the club staff yourself unless your host invites you to do so).
- Do not ask your host (or anyone else on the premises) about membership procedures, dues, who else is a member, etc. The history of the club or its buildings, however, are likely to be a welcome topic of conversation.

On the Tennis Court:

- Wear whites. Even if they aren't deemed mandatory by the club's rule book, they're sure to look fresh and appropriate.
- Don't wear your hat backward, or short shorts.
- Wear tennis sneakers (i.e., those with little or no treads). Sneakers of any other kind will tear up clay or grass courts.
- Always let your host lead going on and off the court.
- Don't chatter during the game. You're there to play.

- If you're a great deal more accomplished than your host, tone down your game to your host's level, and compliment your host on the strong points of his game.

On the Golf Course:

- Dress appropriately. If you are in doubt about anything, ask your host or someone at the facility where you will be playing. (Again, no backward hats or short shorts. Women, Bermuda shorts and golf skirts should be just above the knee, no shorter.)
- A note on vocabulary: You are going to "play golf." You are not "golfing."
- Compliment your host on the facilities and condition of the course. Note how pleased you are to be playing a course you've always wanted to play.
- Stay out of a player's line of sight while he prepares to hit a shot. Don't walk in your opponent's lie on the green, or make noise when he is putting.
- No one cares what your handicap is as long as you play fast.
- Let your host set the bet and the game.
- Be polite (and listen) to caddies: They know the club, players, and rules far better than you do.
- It's a lovely gesture to offer to tip the caddies for yourself and your host. Your host will likely refuse, but if you insist, he will be grateful.
- Men should have a blazer in the car, and both men and women should have long pants, in case you are asked into the clubhouse for a meal.

No matter what the sport, it's important to be a good loser, and a gracious winner. Regardless of the outcome, shake your opponent's hand and say, "Good game."

13 | Stick a Fork in Me

Every now and then I have a really, really long day. When one of these draws to a close, I've been known to turn to my assistant and say, "Stick a fork in me, please—I am *done*." Because she's someone who's worked with me for a while—and knows my many grammar phobias—she finds this funny. (Or perhaps she just pretends to—I recognize grammar humor may not be a knee-slapper for everybody.)

What makes this funny to me, then? Well, the mental image of me as a giant baked potato aside, it's funny because grammatically, "done" is a word that should be applied only to the readiness (or lack thereof) of food. "Finished" is the word you want to include in every other situation. (Okay, I get the joke is not going to crack everybody up. . . .)

While I understand this type of minutiae may seem like just that—minutiae—there's a reason this book is called *The Wow Factor*. Displaying knowledge of these distinctions is the sort of attention to detail that just might impress a superior, making him or her more confident in your ability to step in as their number two should the necessity arise.

What other grammatical booby traps are worth avoiding? The distinction between "can" vs. "may," while incorporated into the children's game, "Mother may I?," appears to have dropped by the wayside for many adults. "Can" is used when there is, in fact, a genuine question as to whether or not something can be accomplished; "may" is used when you're requesting permission.

"Who" vs. "whom" represents an ongoing challenge for many.

"Who" is used when it could be replaced by "he" or "she"; "whom" is used when it can be replaced by "him" or "her." For example, the answer to "Who is here?" is "He is here." "Him" is not. The answer to "To whom should I give this?" is "Give it to him." You don't give it to "he."

"Further" vs. "farther" takes people further into the dilemma, "further" being used when you talk about metaphysical distance, "farther" when it's physical.

"Compliment" and "complement" are often confused. "Compliment" is used when you're offering someone praise—"You did an extraordinary job"—and, perhaps, a drink on the strength of it: "May I offer you a complimentary glass of wine?" "Complement" was what Tom Cruise was referring to when he—famously or infamously—told Renée Zellweger, "You complete me," in his role as Jerry Maguire: It is something that completes or makes perfect a larger whole. So, "A glass of Merlot would complement your steak admirably; it's compliments of the house" is a sentence that would make my heart sing.

"There," "their," and "they're" are regularly jumbled. "There" is used to denote a specific place: "It's over there." "Their" lets others know it doesn't belong to you but to someone else: "It's not mine, it's theirs." And "they're" is a contraction of "they are," as in, "They're on their way over." (Please note the double word score of including "they're" and "their" in that sentence.)

Speaking of contractions, "it's" is a contraction that stands for "it is," while "its" is the possessive form of "it." For example, in "Don't judge a book by its cover," the cover in question belongs to the book.

"Your" and "you're" are frequently interchanged, despite the fact that "your" denotes something that belongs to you—"Is that your book?"—while "you're" is a contraction of "you are," as in, "You're so kind to lend me your book." (Again, note my double word score.)

"Lie" and "lay" are often garbled. "Lie" is used when you want to recline, as in "I need to go lie down." "Lay" is necessary when an object is being placed somewhere—chickens may well lie down to do so, but they lay their eggs.

I draw the line, however, at elucidating piqued vs. peaked (which seems to run rampant in personal ads everywhere), as it does not pique my interest. Should yours have been piqued by the above, however, I recommend picking up a copy of Strunk and White's *Elements of Style*, or Lynne Truss's *Eats, Shoots & Leaves*, as both are guaranteed to not only inform, but amuse.

For the Love of ~~Peat~~ Pete

Since I was on the topic of language, I thought I'd also include a list of frequently misused phrases:

Incorrect	Correct
For all intensive purposes	For all intents and purposes
I'm nauseous	I'm nauseated
Through the ringer	Through the wringer
Do you talk Spanish?	Do you speak Spanish?
That color green	That shade of green
Between you and I	Between you and me
Her and I	She and I
How come. . . . ?	Why is it that . . . ?
A mute point	A moot point
Adverse to	Averse to
A fine tooth comb	A fine-toothed comb
Quite unique/very unique	Unique (something that's unique can't be qualified)
Fiction novel	Novel (a novel is, by definition, a work of fiction)

Again, while it's possible many people will think of this as nitpicking or hairsplitting (would that we had time to delve into those two phrases), mastery of these seemingly small elements can largely impact your future success.

"No Problem" Is One

While I'm busy being picky, I thought I'd also bring up the ubiquitous "No problem," so often used instead of "You're welcome."

Now, I get it. "No problem" does sound infinitely cooler. In fact, you're so cool you didn't even break a sweat making whatever happened happen. That said, it also lives for most listeners in the land of slackerdom: "Hey, dude, no problem." (For the record, "No worries" and "My bad" also live here—it's not a good neighborhood.) It also includes the use of the word "problem," which is not a word most of us respond to with vim and vigor.

Given this, my request would be for you to substitute the somewhat more formal "You're welcome" in those moments when you have, in fact, taken some trouble on another's behalf.

Speaking of slacker vernacular, I will also take this time to request that "yes" replace "yeah" in your vocabulary and to point out that despite the fact that McDonald's might be "*lovin'* it," I, in fact, am not. Neither are those around you who are in the know. Don't drop your g's.

(Mis)Pronunciation(s)

As a child, I was forever mispronouncing words. As was my family's wont, these moments were greeted with shrieks of laughter and calls for others to come hear how I had unwittingly made a mistake—all of which scarred me enough that I can tell you exactly which words I mispronounced, how I mispronounced them, and where I was standing when it happened.

Suffice it to say, there are better ways to correct people.

We've all had moments when we realize we don't know exactly how to say something—or we hear someone say something incorrectly— and it's necessary to speak up. The tricky bit is how.

If you're unsure of a word's pronunciation, I recommend making it everybody's problem. "I don't know if I'm saying this right. Is it X or is it Y?" is a perfectly reasonable question. Another way is to ask: "I've heard the word spelled M-O-R-E-S pronounced a couple of different ways. Do you know which is right?" (NB: The correct pronunciation is actually "morays.")

If you're in the position of having to correct someone, I recommend keeping it very simple if you know the person well. "Actually, that's pronounced X" should do it. If it's someone you don't know well, I recommend asking, "I've always wondered—because I've heard it said both ways—is it X or is it Y?" This should open up enough of a dialogue for somebody to go on dictionary.com and listen to the pronunciation guide.

Another way people go astray is by adding s's to words: "anywheres," "anyways," etc. Again, if it's someone you know well, simply saying "There's no s on that; it's just 'anyway' " should do it. If it's someone you don't know well, I would give it a bit more lead-in: "This is awkward, but I think it's important for me to say. I've noticed you add an s to the end of 'anyway'—you may not realize it, but you say, 'anyways.' It's a small thing, but I wanted to make you aware of it because it's the kind of thing that might trip a grammar alarm in the meeting."

(No Need to) Second That Emotion

Another grammatical misstep I've also been noting is the tendency toward verbal redundancy, seen in phrases such as "This is also a consideration for you, as well," or "I had a mental daydream," or a recent favorite that I heard made by a beloved television pundit, "He seems to be making a judgment in his mind."

Um . . . where else would he make it?

Many of these have crept into our language from K-tel, or at least bad advertising: consider "added extra," "new innovation," and "amazing

marvel." Others are just clichés, pure and simple: "gather together,"
"hoist up," "advance warning," "past history," "recall back," or "repeat
again."

My point is, it's a "true fact" (is there any other kind?) that they are a
"grave danger" (again—any other kind?). Be on the lookout for them in
your speech and your writing. One good way to police yourself is to
review your writing with one of Strunk and White's *Elements of Style*'s
iron rules in mind: "Omit needless words."

"In Other Words"

Another addendum I will caution you against is finishing your point and
then immediately restarting your engine with "In other words . . .," after
which you treat your listener to a slightly revised edition of what you
just said.

In other words, you don't tell people the same thing twice. (You see
how irritating it is?)

Please trust your listener to ask clarifying questions if he or she
hasn't understood.

Sample Script: "This Is She"

Although I detest the land of make-believe, let us pretend for a moment
you have called someone and are waiting for him or her to pick up. Following is the right—and the wrong—way to announce yourself:

Incorrect	Correct
Is this X?	This is Y. May I please speak with X?

Yes, it's true: You need to announce yourself before asking for the person you're trying to reach. Essentially, you've just knocked on her door—it's only polite to say who you are when she opens it.

Additionally, should someone be calling you, your response to "May I please speak with X?" is "This is he" or "This is she." Not "This is him" or "This is her." While this may sound stilted, it's correct.

14 | The Six Layers of Why

The Six Layers of Why is a mental exercise consultants use to make sure they are ready to explain their data, findings, and recommendations to the client. Although asking the same question over and over may initially seem the function of an irritating child, it can lead to unexpected answers or insights and ensures you haven't left any plot holes.

For example, I was recently working on rebranding a client. Part of my remit was to help them attract a more upscale clientele. As I began researching their current language, I found out that they were intent on holding on to a product description that could only be described as down-market. With my eye on the big picture, my first instinct was just to say, "Change it." Asking why they were so attached to it was a secondary impulse. Luckily, I remembered to take my own advice and ask why. Their initial reaction was "It's always been that way." Asking "Why?" several times after that was edifying. The first "Why?" revealed it was because that was the decision made in the 1940s by the founder's son. "Why did he make that decision?" To attract the customers of his day.

With this information in hand, I was able to successfully appeal to their sense of heritage—and to logic—in my request that they change their description so that they could continue their legacy of attracting the customers of *their* day: a decision everyone was comfortable with because we had taken the time to go through the "Why?" process.

In management consulting this style of thinking and presenting is nearly universal, and I make sure that all my clients' presentations can pass it. Here's an example of how it might work for you:

Say that after a few weeks of studying the client's cheese biscuit business and snack industry data, your "top line recommendation" to the client is that they should open a new facility in Wisconsin. Naturally, the client will ask, "Why?"— "Why" number 1. You then are ready with "Because your costs for making cheese biscuits are much higher than your competitors'." When the client asks, "Why? (2)," you respond that the primary ingredient cost in their biscuits is high-quality cheddar cheese. They then might ask, "Why (3) not switch to processed cheese food like our competitors?" to which you might respond, "Because your customers value the all-natural aspects of your biscuits, and cheese food clashes with your brand image." The client then says, "Okay, but why (4) *Wisconsin*?" You respond, "Because it's got lots of small, high-quality cheese producers, so cheese is cheap there." The client then asks, "Why (5) is cheese so cheap in Wisconsin?" You respond, "Because it's 'America's Dairyland.' If you made orange juice, we'd recommend Florida." The client then asks, "By the way, why (6) is Wisconsin 'America's Dairyland'?" Obviously, you don't say, "Because their license plates told me so." Instead, you're ready with "Because Wisconsin's climate and soil make it one of the best places on earth to raise cows." By now you get the point: Never being satisfied with the first—or even the third—answer gives your thinking real depth and builds your confidence, even if your audience usually never gets beyond the first or second "Why?"

The Six Layers of Why is also a great way to have sales representatives prepare to talk to potential clients about the product or service they're selling, as it ensures they won't fall back on useless modifiers (it's great/amazing/incredible only if you tell me *why*) and forces them to articulate elements of the brand story that might have become so familiar to them that they no longer think to mention them.

For example, I work with a skin care company that routinely brings game-changing products to the marketplace—each of which inevitably has several never-before-seen attributes because the science behind its creation is so cutting-edge. In every instance, I want the sales reps to be able to articulate not only the first three whys that make this product so revolutionary, but also to be able to backtrack into why this brand so often makes these breakthroughs: because the doctor behind the line comes out of cancer research. This answer naturally leads to a conversation about the fact that there is a real doctor involved. Why is that important? It's not creation by a conglomerate. In this way, a story about an inanimate object—a face cream—becomes a human story. And we all respond to human.

Finally, the Six Layers of Why is a great way to prepare for a job interview. For example, as you work on the answers to potential questions, a qualification such as "I was nominated four times for Eastern Sales Manager of the Year" would likely jump to mind. Asking yourself the first why elicits, "because I increased sales twenty-three percent." The second why (in effect, how?) probes you to detail how you did that: "I instituted a new approach to talking to customers." The third why gets behind the performance issue you identified. Whys four, five, and six can help you articulate how you plan to add value to your company of choice once your leading-edge-languaged résumé has gotten you in the door.

As you can see, employing the Six Layers of Why is a fast and effective way to address how you can best present yourself in multiple, multifaceted situations. Instilling this structure company-wide ensures that everyone with whom you work has a comprehensive framework for presenting your products and services to their, and your, best advantage.

Why Not

In this day and age of oversharing, or "TMI," I've noticed a few people falling into the habit of offering others far too many wildly inappropriate "whys" behind their actions or decision-making. For example, "Oh, I'm so sorry I was late. I was having a fight with my husband/had to meet with my kid's probation officer/needed to run to the supermarket and pick up some Pepto—that Mexico trip really killed me." (Honest to goodness, I've had clients say all three to me.)

As you can imagine, it's hard to know how—or if—to respond in these moments.

Should you be on the receiving end of such a why, my recommendation is a murmured "I'm so sorry to hear that," followed by a quick change of subject.

Should you find yourself opening your mouth to give someone a why that's simply not critical, I recommend asking yourself, "Is it really necessary to share this information?" If not, close your mouth and move on.

15 | Master the Medium

While it's a bit surprising to me that this essay needs to be put in writing, experience has shown me that there are a number of elements that need to be addressed regarding email addresses.

I'll begin with the most glaring infraction I see, which is: Hotkitty and its ilk, shaft@hotmail.com, etc., are not appropriate email addresses for use in any situation.

"But," I've had people protest, "I just use these with my friends! I would never use them when I'm networking, or interviewing, or in the office." Okay. I believe that you would never consciously choose to use this address in a professional scenario. That said, we all know there are days when we aren't at the top of our game, for whatever reason: We're sleep-deprived, we're checking multiple accounts on our tiny but indispensable PDA, our kid picks up the phone and presses a few buttons when we aren't looking, and suddenly the email's out there and we've added to the joys of our day the fun of cleaning up an interpersonal gaffe that simply didn't have to happen.

Given this, I recommend closing down any accounts you may have with suggestive, cute, silly, personal monikers. While I'm certain this makes me sound like the world's worst killjoy, that's a title I'm willing to own. (Though I would not, of course, set myself up as killjoy@yahoo.com).

Additionally, I'm not a fan of obscure combinations of letters and numbers. While it might be immediately apparent to you, and a helpful aide-mémoire, that your address is your initials and your birthday or your anniversary or some such, you are making others work too hard to remember it. And, as we've learned, when you make me work too hard I feel stupid, and when I feel stupid, I don't like you.

What then, do I recommend you do? My suggestion would be to buy your name as a dot.com. For example, I own francesjones.com, francescjones.com, francescolejones.com, plus the myriad addresses used for my books and my business. Why? Because linking your email to a service that is used by millions of others (Gmail, AOL, Road Runner, etc.) doesn't leave the impression of you as unique — as a force to be reckoned with. Buying your name tells others you take yourself seriously, and they need to, too. With this in hand, should your name be John Doe you can set yourself up as John@johndoe.com. This can be done at sites such as www.register.com, or www.networksolutions.com.

And, while we're on the subject of formality and informality on the World Wide Web, I am going to request you clean up your MySpace/Facebook/Twitter, etc. page. Because although I have no doubt your trip to Vegas with your friends was memorable (or memorable now that you've posted the pictures online), these should not be available for the world to see — and thinking the world isn't going to look is, in this day and age, laughable. As many of you know who read publications from *The Wall Street Journal* to the *New York Post*, job candidates across any number of industries — from bankers to police officers — have been weeded out due to inappropriate postings on these personal pages. Also consider that the latest vetting form for the White House requires candidates to list "all aliases or 'handles' you have used to communicate on the Internet"; everything they've written, "including, but not limited to, any posts or comments on blogs or other websites"; links to their Facebook or MySpace pages; and any potentially embarrassing "electronic communication, including but not limited to an email, text message or instant message." But it's not just White House jobs — in fact, in addition to their checking your pages on their own time, recently I've heard stories of potential employers asking you to open your Facebook page mid-interview. I sincerely hope that gave you pause.

How am I classifying "inappropriate?" Any postings referencing the intimate details of your personal relationship, your GI tract, or your mental health; and any photos in which you are drinking, smoking, leering, sneering, suggestively posed, or otherwise indisposed. If you are in doubt, I recommend asking yourself the following question: "Does this entry/picture make me sound/look like I can be trusted with one hundred thousand dollars?" If it doesn't, get rid of it. These portals are your public face — or shop window — to the world. You wouldn't want to run into the HR director with whom you just interviewed scantily clad, slightly inebriated, or making lewd gestures with your friends on the street; don't let him or her find you that way on your home page.

Eye Spy

As a kid, one of my best-loved books was *Harriet the Spy*. As part of her spy technique, Harriet carried a notebook wherever she went and wrote down everything she overheard. Those things she didn't understand, she asked about. Among my favorite moments was when Harriet asked her father what "I've had it" meant. To which he responded, "Had it? Had it?? It just means tired."

But while many of us will happily spend hours on the Web doing copious amounts of research to prepare for our vacation, track down the foreign exchange student we knew in eleventh grade, or research the tickle we've had in the back of our throat for a week, we are less inclined to do a fast, in-and-out check on a vocabulary word or industry term we don't know when we bump into it in our day-to-day conversation. In fact, the practice of actively researching these words and phrases usually sounds like, "Well, I'm not a hundred percent sure, but I think it means X. . . ."

The trouble with this approach is that every now and then you might find yourself using a word in a way that undermines the point you're trying to make, as one of my clients did recently when referring to something as "infinitesimal," her perception being that because it contained the word "infinite" it meant large, when, in fact, it means tiny. . . . This didn't end well.

So what do I recommend?

Well, in addition to the notebook technique employed by Harriet, one of my more book-loving clients went out and bought a cookbook stand. That's right: a cookbook stand. Then, he got out his old, heavy Collegiate dictionary, set it up in a prominent place in his office, and promised himself that every time he encountered a word with which he wasn't familiar he was going to look it up.

A slightly less ponderous option is bookmarking www.dictionary.com on your computer, an alternative that has the added advantage of allowing you to listen to how the word is pronounced, since you're more likely to use it if you feel comfortable knowing how it's said. This site also has a free Word of the Day email you can sign up for.

Another fantastic, free tool, should you wish to actively expand your vocabulary, is signing up for www.wordsmith.org—whose capacity to introduce me to words I have never come across never ceases to amaze. (If you're skeptical, consider some recent entries alone: "subintelligitur," "quodlibet," and "infundibuliform.") In addition to signing myself up, I have signed up a number of my clients, and it's been one of my most popular gifts.

In addition to their having an intermittently tenuous grasp on general vocabulary, another thing I've noticed as I move from industry to industry is that people sometimes don't have a complete grasp of the technical terms of their industry. They'll hear a word or phrase used over and over and—because everyone else in the room seems familiar with it—they'll let the fact that they don't quite know what it means go by. This is particularly common in industries where new phrasing is constantly being coined to keep up with trends in the field: for example, the use of "charticle" in magazine publishing to denote an article appearing in chart form, or "tryvertising" in marketing, to describe the trend of allowing users to experience the product before they leave the store—brilliantly exemplified by Apple's Mac stores.

If you've found yourself in this situation, I would recommend making

an immediate note of anything you hear with which you are unfamiliar—
in your notebook, your PDA, on the stickies function of your computer—
and looking it up posthaste. You might also make a point of not only
reading the magazines geared to your trade, but taking one week to
write down every single term you see that you aren't a hundred percent
sure you could define for someone else, and finding out exactly what it
means.

This type of active research is particularly important should you have
recently switched career paths and need to get up to speed quickly on
new vocabulary, acronyms, or industry shorthand. In these instances, I
would keep a list of anything you hear that's unfamiliar or unclear, work
to define it yourself, and then ask your boss or an established colleague
for fifteen minutes of their time during which you can say, "This is the
list I've made of terms that are new to me. This is what I think they
mean. Am I defining them as you—or the industry—would?"

16 | Sign with Style

"Dear Folks" and "Warm Best" were the particular opening and closing choices of our father's estate attorney after my dad's death. While there may, in fact, be times when they are appropriate, this wasn't one of them—it was more hoedown than heartening, and left me asking myself, "Why am I paying three hundred dollars an hour to someone whose craft involves language but who opens a letter 'Dear Folks'?" I wanted an estate lawyer, not Grizzly Adams.

What's another troubling greeting example? Here's one that landed recently in my in-box, sent to me from a medical supplier. "*Hi, X here with Y company. I'll keep this short, since it's just after we're all getting back to work, but my partner and I are on a bit of a mission. Anyway . . .*"

Ummmm . . . where shall I start?

- "X here" is more suited to my morning drive-time disc jockey than to my medical supplier. While dull, my preference would be "Dear Frances." Yes, configuring a mass email so it appears personal is a chore, but lots of people are doing it. I recommend you do too.

- Grammar problems aside, I'm not digging on the idea that anyone who supplies others with medical equipment takes time off from work—they very well may, and probably should, but I don't want to hear about it. "I know you're just back from your holiday, so I'll be brief" would be both more effective and more confidence-inspiring.

- To me, you are either on a mission or you aren't; "a bit of a mission" is like being "a bit pregnant." Enough said.

- As for ending their opening with "Anyway. . . ." Well, words fail even me.

Am I being too particular? I don't think so. In both these examples, the writers' choice to go folksy undermined the importance of what they had to offer: Neither estate law nor medical supply is an overtly ha-ha field of work. And while there is a market for down-home, as evidenced by the abundance of "Ye Olde Shoppes" (I am irresistibly reminded of the *Simpsons* episode that placed a sign outside the Cider Mill saying, "Now 40% Quainter!"), we're on a razor's edge these days—why put yourself at a disadvantage when it's so easy to do it right?

So, what to do? If you have just arrived at a company and no style guide has been offered to you, note both the salutations and the sign-offs of your superiors and follow suit. (Provided, of course, that they do not include slang, foreign affectations along the lines of "Ciao" or "Cheers," or constructions along the lines of "Warm best.") If you're making a choice for yourself, I think it's hard to go wrong with "Sincerely," "Best," or "Regards." I would also ask that quotes of the day, emoticons, and the like never, ever appear, as these detract from others' ability to take you seriously.

Speaking of company style guides, an offer to put one together—while I guarantee it will be maddening to produce—will be very gratefully received. What might you think about including? As noted, I would have standardized salutations and closes. I would have guidelines for how people's titles and contact information should be handled. I would have a company-approved typeface chosen, and I would put in writing any policies regarding personalizing emails. Should the company have a tagline, brand promise, holophrase, logo, wordmark, or seal that appears with its name, I would provide guidelines as to how it should appear. The beauty of a document of this kind is twofold: It ensures company-wide consistency, and it sends a message that no detail is too small to be taken seriously. For example, here is a guide I offered one of my clients:

Email Guidelines:

Email is probably the most common means of handling routine correspondence. Email messages are considered less formal than written correspondence in letter or memo form. However, email messages should be professional and consistent in content, tone, and appearance. Remember, too, that emails get forwarded: Always uphold the standards of our brand in everything you send.

In addition to those general standards, the following specific standards apply to all emails:

- Avoid using graphic elements in email messages. Graphic elements add significantly to the size of email files and seldom add significantly to the value of the content.

- Use standard typefaces in email messages. Times New Roman or Arial are preferred for use in body copy. Please note that the sender's name should not be in a font that simulates a handwritten "signature": It should be in the standard message font.

- Do not use sayings, slogans, icons, or quotations in your email signature.

Email signature format:

You should create an email signature to "sign" all email messages. It should contain your name, title, and appropriate contact information in the following format:

First Name, Last Name

Title and Function

Mailing/Office Address

Telephone Number
(including extension, if any)

Cell Number

Fax Number

Email Address

Business URL

Pedantic? Possibly. But what I discovered when it was presented was that of the several hundred people sending email from that business, each had "personalized" his or her email in some way. Putting this in writing ensured consistency across the board.

Finally, two additional thoughts, from the commonsensical to the sublime:

If you don't know the correct form of address for the person to whom you're writing—or if there is a question in your mind as to whether they might like "Ms." vs. "Mrs." or "Mr." vs. no honorific at all—call his or her assistant and inquire. If you're feeling inspired to learn more, consider picking up *Debrett's New Guide to Etiquette and Modern Manners*, which has a fifteen-page appendix devoted to nothing else but correct forms of address, including—should you need it—the correct way to address an envelope to an alderman, open a letter to a circuit judge, verbally address a bishop, and what the place card for a viscount should say.

URGENT!!

Speaking of first impressions, I wanted to take a moment to talk about email subject lines—another place I've noticed a certain amount of "tone deafness," with entries ranging from far too familiar/vague to far too demanding.

Let's begin with URGENT, and its alternative CRISIS. Here's what I know: The word "crisis" rarely moves things along. In fact, it generally ratchets up everyone's blood pressure without producing a discernibly different result; additionally, when it's used too often people no longer pay attention to the note—or the opinion expressed. As noted in *How to Wow*, my request is that you use "situation," not "crisis." With regard to "urgent," I'm now requesting that before you use it, you ask yourself, "Is this as urgent to the receiver as it is to me?" (The same question should be asked before hitting the "priority" setting on the email itself—which gives your email a little flag, special color, etc., again, "priority" for whom?) If it isn't, my recommendation would be to have a subject line that relates to the note you're sending; in the body copy of that note, you can say, "As you can imagine, I'm hoping to resolve this/get an answer sooner rather than later." You can also (gasp) call the person, underscoring the sense of urgency.

What are some other headings guaranteed to set my teeth on edge? How about:

- For when you get in on Monday

   Unless you're my boss, why are you dictating my Monday activity? (We won't even get into why you're emailing me on a weekend. . . .)

- Just so I don't forget/Please remind me

   Again, am I your assistant? If you need to make a note to yourself to remind someone of something, feel free. But don't put it in their in-box to get it out of yours.

- Please call me

I understand this one somewhat. You'd like to speak with someone and don't want to interrupt her day. That said, I think leaving her a message in the medium in which you want to continue the conversation is best. In these circumstances, then, I would recommend leaving a message on her voice mail, and if you're still feeling like double-teaming her, sending her an email saying you've left her a message and asking if she can call at her convenience.

• I know you're out sick but . . .

Um, yes. I'm out sick. Your life is not more important than mine.

At the opposite extreme are overly vague headlines along the lines of "Friday?" or "Your thoughts?" or simply "?" (I admit I'm guilty of the last. . . .) In every case, I would prefer (and will now make a habit of myself) spelling out exactly what you're trying to clarify, so "Friday?" becomes "Friday meeting. Your office at 11?"; "Your thoughts?" becomes "Request for feedback for Monday's report"; and "?" has a reference included to the question you will be asking.

The other subject-line misdirect I've noticed comes from people who write to you simply by searching their old emails for the last email that *you* wrote (which may have had the subject "Appointment May 12th, 2 PM?"), hitting the "reply" key, and then merrily writing you about a totally different matter. Don't do this. Cut and paste the email address into a fresh email, and have the subject line of your email actually reflect the subject—like not keeping people waiting, it shows respect for other people's time and mental energy.

Texting—Time Out

Ah, texting. The immediacy of the medium, combined with the breathless way it's often used to impart urgency to television shows lacking drama based on human interaction (or skillful writing), seems to have infected everyone with a bizarre sense of urgency and entitlement—one that doesn't translate well outside the 90210 television zip code.

For example, one of my clients recently received a text that began "Heads Up!" from a vendor with whom she was to be meeting *for the first time.* The remainder of the text read as follows: "I just want to give you a heads up that I may be 10–15 mins late I'm stuck in traffic." While letting someone know you are running late is an admirable impulse, how that information is conveyed is just as important as conveying it. In this instance, if it truly wasn't possible to speak *to* her because he'd forgotten his hands-free phone headset, the vendor could have sent a text message that read, "Running 15 minutes late. My apologies. I'm stuck in traffic."

That said, unless the situation is extremely urgent, text-messaging is not an appropriate way to communicate in a professional setting. Just because someone gave you her cell number doesn't mean this is how it should be used to reach her. Should you truly find yourself with no alternative, please spell out all the words. (It goes without saying that you should save the winking, smiling, giggling, frowning, laughing, party-throwing, etc., emoticons for your friends.) I guarantee that any additional charge you might incur on your phone bill is money well spent.

17 | The Must-Have FAQ

A few years ago, I spent a year rebranding a client's firm: name, logo, corporate culture . . . every element was in the mix. Among our most important work was putting together a set of "frequently asked questions"—and their answers—for both external stakeholders (customers, suppliers, and partners) and their employees. Why did I consider this so important? Because this organization had grown rapidly with the result that a lot of information that people who had been there for years thought "everybody" knew or was "obvious" about the business was big news to the outfit's ever-shifting and growing staff. This, of course, meant that its customers were missing out too.

The same is likely true for you. In the same way you need to have an "elevator speech" about yourself, your idea/product, or your business—a package of words that clearly and memorably conveys the essence of yourself, your firm, or your passion to the CEO or potential client with whom you unexpectedly share a thirty-second elevator ride—you need to have clearly articulated answers to the frequently asked questions (FAQs) that you, your ideas/products, or your business receive: answers to questions about what you believe in/your mission, what your unique value-added is, and who you are not (and why). These should be designed not only to convey what you want to *tell* quickly and easily, but also to convey what most people want to *know* about you, your business, or your idea (hopefully, there's a lot of overlap here; only the most egotistical people think that they're indistinguishable) in language that's precise, colorful, and concise.

With this in mind, here are three questions applicable to any business, to which you should have memorable, considered answers, whether in a pitch meeting, at an industry conference, or on the golf course:

1. What's your brand promise?

   The answer to this not only addresses your values, but explains how your adherence to those values is going to make your customer's life better/easier. For example, if you work in high-end frozen food you might say, "Your health is our first priority, so we are committed to using only organic ingredients in our products."

   Why does this particular answer work? Well, as was noted in *How to Wow*, "you" is the most persuasive word in the English language, according to a Yale University study, so beginning a sentence with it automatically helps people hear it better. If your answer was simply "We are committed to using only organic ingredients," it's unlikely you would catch your listener's attention in the same way.

   Another option might be to acknowledge the concerns uppermost in everyone's minds. For example, if you work in telecommunications you might say, "In these times we understand it's critical for you to be able to stay in touch with your employer, your network, your loved ones; with this in mind, we committed ourselves to providing you with twenty-four-hour customer support."

   The other beauty of this answer is that it doesn't end, "we committed ourselves to providing *our customers* with twenty-four-hour support." Why? Because using "customers" in this context makes your listeners or readers feel like you're talking to a constituency that exists in a petri dish. Saying "you" reassures them you are talking directly to them.

2. What's your best selling product/idea? Why?

   You will, of course, know your bestselling product. (If you don't, please remedy that posthaste.) The "why?" here should tell a story about why or how your product makes your listener's life better or easier. (FYI: This does not include useless modifiers such as "great/amazing/wonderful," etc.) So, for example, if you work for a skin care company, your moisturizer isn't "amazing," it "protects against sun damage, reduces redness, and smooths away fine lines."

3. Who is your biggest competition? (Or its softball alternative, Oh, so you're like X?—the competitor with whom you're most frequently confused, for all the wrong reasons.)

Your answer to this one should not name names—why give your competition free advertising? Instead, I recommend, "To compete is to imitate. There are some companies that have similar products, but none have the X, Y, Z features that ours does."

You will also want to have answers to softball questions, such as:

1. What is it, exactly, that you do?

In my case, the answer I've worked out to this one is "I help people like you look and sound their best during TV interviews and in boardroom meetings. For example, I recently worked with a client who . . ." An answer of this kind reassures/reminds the people with whom I'm speaking that my services are for them as well, and giving them an example helps my answer stick in their memory.

If you work in an industry such as insurance, real estate, or banking, you don't want to assume people understand exactly what that means, or that they have your grasp of industry vocabulary. Alternatively, you don't want them to associate you with a negative experience they might have had with someone else in your field, so it's important to include a story in which you and/or your business excelled. With this in mind, your answer to a question of this kind might be "I work in commercial real estate—renting and selling space to midsized businesses. For example, do you know that great old building they just restored on the corner of X? Well, we were the ones who helped Y get their foot in the door. . . ." Circling your answer around to something people interact with daily allows them to ground you and what you do in a world they're familiar with.

2. What makes you unique/different/better?

"We stand out because of our commitment to/belief in/the quality of our X, Y, Z." Again, your answer here must be grounded in how your company or brand's qualities and features are going to make your listeners'/readers' life better. At the end of the day, they aren't concerned about you. They want to know what's in it for them.

3. Who's your dream customer?

The best way I've found to think about this answer is to think of it almost as a personal ad, as this is a useful tool for enticing the "armchair buyer." For example, if you're in the business of selling sunglasses, you might say, "If you're someone who appreciates quality, this choice is great for you, as you get full-spectrum eye protection in a fashion-forward package."

Hmmm . . . Are you saying if I buy these I'm smart, healthy, and fashionable? I'll take two.

Finally, you will want to have answers to the questions you most dread getting:

1. How's business been for you in this economy?

Unless business has been booming, the key to this answer is to balance optimism with recognition of reality. So, for example, you might say, "Well, our president said 'a crisis is a terrible thing to waste'—and that's been our mind-set. We've certainly seen a lot of changes, but we're balancing that by working harder and smarter. For example . . .," at which point you might tell a story about some cost-cutting you've done, a creative way you've found to reach out to customers, a moment when your team's loyalty surprised you, etc. The thing you don't want to do is to begin with "It's been tough, but . . .," as there's no guarantee the person asking will listen beyond those first three words.

2. Weren't you the ones who "masterminded" last year's "growth strategy?" What happened?

Here, your answer needs to be direct and nonconfrontational. Given this, you might say, "We were the architects behind that strategy, and here's what we were thinking. . . ." Filling people in on the backstory behind your decision-making allows them to both feel like an insider and do some Monday-morning quarterbacking. Although it can be difficult, I recommend smiling and agreeing with whatever they come back with, as it's unlikely you'll change their mind by pointing out the flaws in their ideas or logic.

Please bear in mind that your tonality and physicality are going to be critical with this answer. As I said in How to Wow, when answering confrontational questions the best thing you can do is to channel your inner New York popular-restaurant hostess—the one who comes over with a big smile, touches your arm, and says, "Your table's going to be another half an hour . . ." so nicely that it takes you a moment to figure out you're not getting what you want.

3. You're expensive—are you worth it?

The answer to this needs to begin unequivocally, then acknowledge the questioner's concern, after which you can enumerate your, your product's, or your service's features and benefits. So, it might look like "Yes, we are. While I understand it may seem like a great deal of money, here's what you're getting for your investment: X, Y, Z."

For example, one of my clients is a designer whose line includes extremely expensive T-shirts. The way we handled his price was by pointing out that yes, your average T-shirt costs X amount but had to be replaced every six months because it couldn't hold up to repeated washings—his could; that his shirts were so well cut you could wear them under suits, thus saving on dry cleaning; and that his colors and cotton were so lovely, you'd end up wearing his shirts twice as often as any others you might have in your closet.

With these answers in hand, you can make decisions about where and to whom they should be made available. In my experience, an FAQ one-sheet detailing answers to all the information publicly available, as well as in-house answers to the tougher questions, should be part of every company handbook; an FAQ page on your website should be a mandatory feature; and anytime you are headed into a large event or tricky situation, answers to any potentially disquieting questions should be worked out and disseminated to all key personnel prior to their engaging with their teams or the outside world.

18 | It's All in the Timing

"Timing: the alpha and omega of aerialists, jugglers, actors, diplomats, publicists, generals, prizefighters, revolutionists, financiers, dictators, lovers."

Marlene Dietrich didn't speak often, but in this instance it was worth waiting for, because although most of us pay lip service to the idea of "waiting until the time is right," we also live in a culture of immediate gratification, which I believe has thrown off our sense of timing. And nowhere is this more common than in our speech—a place where many of us struggle with how much or how little to say, and how and when to say it.

I think this is because we do so much of our communicating electronically that we're no longer sensitive to the delicate interplay of a well-choreographed conversation: the give-and-take, the pauses to calculate and recalibrate, the sometimes-necessary silence. In our unease, we find ourselves saying too much or too little, too meekly or too aggressively.

Two distinct arenas in which I've seen my clients struggle are in the pauses necessary for a successful negotiation, and in the verbal thrust and parry that goes into the art of interrupting. Let's look first at the power of the pause:

Using Silence to Persuade:

Often, one of our strongest tactics in persuading others is silence, not speech. Speaking from my own experience, I learned this as a parks officer was ruminating on whether to write me a ticket for $50 or

$100. It seemed I was due for the $100 ticket, as my dog had been both on the dog-free lawn and off his leash. In that moment, I considered saying that he hadn't, in fact, been off his leash—he'd been running about dragging his leash with him. I suspect, however, that pointing this out would have landed me the $100 ticket, instead of the $50 one I ultimately got. Thankfully, I remembered in time that a) my sense of humor doesn't always translate for others, b) silence is powerful, and c) most people are on our side if we give them time to be. How can you put this to use? Well, the next time you need to ask someone to take notes for you in a meeting, cover for you on a Saturday, or, possibly, be lenient about writing you a ticket, I recommend making your request, giving the reason why you're making it, and Then. Saying. Nothing. This is the tricky bit. Too often, we keep rephrasing our reason, or coming up with fresh ones, leaving the person feeling harried or bullied, and thus, less inclined to help us out. Asking and then (pause) waiting for the answer is more likely to get you the result you're seeking.

Using Silence to Sell:

The value of silence is also in play in a sales scenario—a statement that might initially seem counterintuitive, as many of us share a mental caricature of a fast-talking car salesman. But despite the fact that many salespeople begin with a rhetorical question along the lines of "Are you happy with your current choice?" or "Is there anything you think would serve you better?," they rarely wait more than two to three seconds after asking before rephrasing the question, answering it themselves, or changing the subject. Research has shown, however, that decision-makers need *eight to ten seconds* to think of the beginning of their answer—and that as they speak they come up with more ideas. Given this, the longer you allow someone else to think, rather than trying to do the thinking for him, the likelier you are to get your product or idea adopted.

Using Silence to Negotiate:

Another place silence can be useful is during salary negotiations. Recently, one of my clients told me a story of going in to negotiate a freelance fee for working with a nonprofit organization rather than the banks with whom he had formerly done business. Under the circumstances, he didn't feel comfortable naming his usual rate—particularly as he really needed the work. Given that, he'd made the reluctant decision to be willing to drop his number by a third. Therefore, he opened with, "My usual rate is X," but before he could get to, "but because you're not a bank I'm prepared to blah, blah . . .," his interviewer said, "That sounds fair." His takeaway? Name your number and then stop talking. As with letting the seller sell himself, let your negotiator do his own negotiating.

The Art of Interrupting:

Another place I find that my clients struggle with verbal give-and-take is when someone interrupts them. They're also frequently confounded by when and how to interrupt someone else—an almost more difficult situation.

I agree that this particular verbal dance can be tricky: sometimes because we don't want to seem pushy, or rude; sometimes because we have a strong aversion to doing to someone else what we hate having done to ourselves; sometimes because we simply get overwhelmed, and abandoning the conversation is easier than slogging through it. All of these reactions are valid, and I will give you techniques for handling each. But before I do, I want to look at one way that many of us have been interrupting for years without knowing it—a situation that, for reasons beyond the scope of this book, is more common to women than to men. I call it the noninterruption interruption.

"Of Course!" AKA "Woman Interruptus":

What I've noticed is that women are prone to agreeing and encouraging while others are speaking. "Of course," we'll say, "absolutely." Or, "I know exactly what you mean!"

The trouble with this is that it can, in fact, either cause people to lose their train of thought, or—if you're speaking with someone who's naturally more reticent—have them pull back into themselves so you can tell your story.

What would I have you do instead? My recommendation is that you signal your encouragement and agreement via nonverbal techniques: Lean in, nod your head, smile.

"Hang on . . .":

Having taken care not to interrupt others how, then, should you handle someone who has interrupted you? While there is a certain levity to "That was a comma, not a period," it's also true that it can land badly.

Given this, my recommendation would be "Hang on. I know you're anxious to make your point—and of course I want to hear it—but I wasn't quite finished." Acknowledging the other person's need to speak ensures they don't end up feeling rebuked. If you can do it with a certain amount of levity, I applaud you. At the very least, please don't put your hand in their face like a school crossing guard. *How to Wow* opened with the 7/38/55 statistic supplied by Dr. Albert Mehrabian for a reason (people only remember 7 percent of the words you say; 38 percent of your impact comes from your tonal quality; 55 percent from what your body is doing while you're speaking)— it seems we are far more sensitive to *how* something is said than to *what* is said. This idea needs to be at the forefront of your consciousness when handling interruptions. Although your temperature—and your temper—is likely rising, you need to pause, inhale, and speak on an exhalation. You need to keep your tone even (if you can't keep it light) and you need to keep your body from contracting. Yes, you are on defense, but once you're in a crouch, the other person will be too.

Chronic Interruptus:

Everybody has been in a meeting with someone who's a chronic interrupter—you know who I mean: the person who waits no more than a few words into your response before once again beginning to talk over you. If you find yourself in that situation, and the above tactic has not worked, I offer the following. (Please note, however: I recommend its use only for those who can't seem to let you finish a thought.) In these situations, the magic phrase is "I'm getting the impression you don't think I'm listening to you." When they say, "Why?" your response is "Because you keep interrupting me."

The beauty of this particular phrasing is that it doesn't directly accuse the person of cutting you off. Instead, it opens with you taking the onus on yourself—you are getting the impression, but they are free to deny it's so. Whether they do or don't, however, I'm quite sure they will check their interruptions as you proceed.

"May I?" No:

Finally, let's look at what to do when you need to interrupt someone else—a not-uncommon scenario when you're running a meeting that's gone off track or are overseeing a team that's gotten into a wrangle.

When this occurs, many of us interject a meek "May I interrupt you?" The trouble with this particular choice is that it doesn't carry the necessary heft to stop the person in his tracks. With this in mind, I'd like to offer the following suggestion for how to step in:

First, I'd ask you to begin by saying, "I'm going to interrupt you"—a choice which ensures your control of the remainder of the conversation. Obviously, your tone is going to matter a lot here: You can make the delivery as heavy or light as the situation warrants. After that, you might go on to say, "This sounds like an important idea, but I don't know that everyone here needs to be in on the discussion—can you and I set another time to discuss it?" Or, "I don't know that that level of detail is required here, but maybe you can follow up with Jane tomorrow?" Again, in this moment, your physicality and tonality are going to be critical: My request is that you sound both firm and encouraging. The goal is to make it seem an interruption in the conversation much the same way halftime is an interruption in sports—you're merely the umpire marking a pause so the combatants can regroup and move forward more effectively.

As you can see, none of the above situations entails a particularly easy form of give-and-take. Each of them, as Dietrich noted, necessitates the timing of *aerialists, jugglers, actors, diplomats* . . . all of whom need to have far more control of their bodies than their words in order to achieve their objectives. Exhibiting physical finesse in concert with your verbal finesse ensures that you, too, will be able to turn interruptions from intrusions into art, and silence from stagnation into success.

19 | Human Resources: An Insider's Guide

There are few things more bewildering than the rituals of a corporate human resources department. Despite the fact that everyone's got one, no two seem to operate along the same lines, and everybody's got a story to tell. With this in mind, I thought I would collect the solutions to a number of issues I've come across in my years of prepping people for job interviews: everything from how to format your résumé to emphasize your strengths and submit it in such a way that you don't piss people off, to how to answer the all-pervasive "What's your greatest strength/weakness?" question (and its sneaky follow-up, "Can you tell me another?"), to how to tackle the perspiration-provoking "Solve this case study" request.

Setting Up Your Résumé:

There are two possible types of résumés you can offer: the chronological and the skills-based. My recommendation is to use the skills-based one if you have a patchy work history or are returning to work after a break; if you're changing careers and want to emphasize transferable skills; if you don't want to look like a job-hopper; or if you are applying for a job that requires skills that you have but haven't used in a while. These résumés group your work under headings such as "Marketing," "Team Building," "Strategy," etc.—all of which can appear under the heading "Overview of Experience." That said, if you use one, be ready to give a clear job chronology in interviews.

Submitting Your Résumé:

What I've observed myself, and had corroborated by HR, is that we tend to name our résumé "Résumé.doc" for purposes of finding it in our system. While this works beautifully for us—most of us have only one résumé—it's utterly irritating to the HR professional receiving hundreds of these a day, who then have to take the time to rename them and delete the original. In all frankness, this is usually when they delete your file entirely. With this in mind, my suggestion would be to name your résumé "Your Name.Résumé.Month Year.doc." So, for example, mine would be "Frances Jones.Résumé.September 2009.doc."

Your Greatest Strength/Weakness:

Once their résumé has gotten applicants in the door, most of them know the importance of having an example in hand for a question along the lines of "What's your greatest strength/weakness?" or "Tell me about a time when you made a mistake/solved a problem." The trouble is that so do HR directors nationwide. Consequently, directors everywhere have begun to follow up their first request with "That sounds great. Can you give me another example?"

Since they know you've prepped, let's outprep them.

As you know, any example of your greatest weakness is just one of your strengths taken to an extreme: You're just so darn persistent, you don't know when to give up. Or you're just so fascinated by your subject that you tend to want to include every detail. If you're speaking about making a mistake or solving a problem, your focus is on the lesson you learned, or, as they say in HR-speak, "the fall that made it possible to stand." For example, "In retrospect, it's easy to see how a different choice would have been a better fit for the situation; the positive outcome, however, is that this reinforced the value of being accountable for my decisions and showed me I have the stamina to regroup and rebuild when things don't go my way."

Now that you have those under your belt, let's look at how and why your round-two answers should build on them:

First, you want to make it seem like your interviewers' second request for an example surprised you, as it will make them feel far more sparkly and make your considered answer that much more effective—having a completely different, pat response might mean they tune you out or write you off. Given this, I recommend having your second response be an extension of your first. So, your second response to the query about your greatest weakness might sound like "Well, when I think about being persistent, one thing I've learned is that if you're going to keep following up with a potential client you can't take rejection personally—in fact, it really helps to keep a sense of humor. For example, when I found myself calling this guy for the fifth time the other day, I prefaced it with, 'Well, since this is my fifth call, I'm pretty sure we're going steady.' " If you were to tackle the "lesson learned," you might go with: "One thing I learned about coming back from a situation like that was that getting my team back on board—making sure I was accountable to them, and allowing them to offer me feedback—was as important as cleaning up the public outcome of my decision. Internal trust is as critical to success as external trust."

Once you've worked out the verbal elements of your answer, I recommend practicing every aspect of the interview with a friend. Yes, I understand it's excruciating—as has been mentioned before, I am not a fan of make-believe—but your delivery is as important as your answers. In this particular case, if you jump right into your second response, it's going to seem canned, whereas if you take a moment to think about it, it's more likely to be taken at face value.

What other nonverbal elements should you consider? As noted in *How to Wow*, you want to be sitting up and forward in your chair. You want to pause before answering each question, inhale, and speak on an exhalation to give your voice resonance and authority, and you don't want to begin speaking until the interviewer is looking at you, not at your résumé.

Since you have them where you want them, you might as well enjoy it.

The Case Interview:

Finally, the "case interview" interview:

Case interviews are standard techniques to select candidates at consulting firms, business schools, software companies, banks, and customer service positions—in short, professional, collegial environments. In general, they come in three types and are designed to prove that you are, indeed, the creative and logical thinker your résumé claims you are, or that you're the "people person" your recommenders claim you can be.

A key thing to remember with all three types is that there is no "right" answer to the case being presented. These are behavioral tests that check mental agility.

Group Case Interviews:

These are more about not failing than about wowing people. They have one goal: to find out which people work and play well with others, who's collegial and able to make an impact in a tactful way in a group setting. So while you definitely want to demonstrate that you can contribute, you don't want to dominate the group's discussion or attempt to take charge in an aggressive way. One of my clients had the experience of being in a group of eight people tasked with deciding whether an American chain restaurant should expand into Asia. They were given half an hour and a whiteboard and told to come up with a yes/no answer and a bulleted list explaining why. Of the eight, three failed—two because they didn't speak, and one because he couldn't stop telling everyone why his idea was right. If you are in this situation, I recommend the following techniques:

- Be the quiet organizer. Suggest that everyone take the first four minutes to read the case, and offer to keep time.

- Suggest something constructive or share any insights that you have.

- If you have no insights, ask people clarifying questions about their ideas.

- Be respectful of anything anyone else contributes, no matter what you may think of it.

- Follow directions. (I know it seems insane that I have to write that, but experience has shown me I do. For example, if you're told, "Only use what you've got," don't offer to look something up on your BlackBerry.)

Bottom line: Be a team player who contributes respectfully to the goal and you'll be fine.

Individual Case Interviews:

In these you *can* wow. But, again, it's not going to be because you got the right answer. Sometimes presented in written form and sometimes out loud, these questions cover a wide range. For instance, they may be "big thinking" questions. For example, one of my clients was asked what he would do about the environment if he were president of a country. His first clarifying question: "On Earth as a whole, or are we considering space exploration?" (At that point, he knew he had them), or they may be brainteasers. Another client was asked why manhole covers were round. (FYI: so cables don't get caught on any corners.) Or they may be practical tasks. When confronted with any of them, keep the following in mind:

- Use all the time they give you.

- Make notes/use paper—particularly if a question is orally delivered.

- If they say you can ask clarifying questions, do, but don't fish too much: Show that you can be content working with the facts you have.

- As you lay out your answer, state your assumptions.

- Stay cool, even if you make a mistake in the arithmetic. All is not lost; they are looking at logic flow.

- Not all the information may by relevant, but don't say, "That's irrelevant." You may be wrong. If you think it's irrelevant, just don't draw on it in your answer.

Again, the point is never that they are asking you the question because no one in their office can figure out the answer—they want to see if you can think logically and clearly under pressure. Approach them like a doctor trying to figure out symptoms and you'll be fine. If you want to do more research, check out www.acethecase.com or www.quintcareers.com/case_interviews.html.

If you're more in a movie mood, check out www.mckinsey.com/careers/how_do_i_apply/how_to_do_well_in_the_interview.aspx.

Simulation Cases:

For these, you are likely being offered cases about the industry in which you'll be working. For customer service positions, they will test how you handle complaints. For sales, they will give you a sample sales situation. For example, one of my clients was put in a room and asked to make three cold calls while being recorded. In these moments, a key thing to remember is not to joke about the situation or problem (I know it sounds obvious as you read it, but some people do relieve tension this way) and to show that you can follow the rules and live up to whatever the company's values happen to be: If they stress customer satisfaction, make sure the customer is satisfied; if they stress efficiency, keep an eye on your time, etc. The U.S. Postal Service has a great test for finding out if people can follow directions: They put everyone in a room, hand them a multiple-choice test, then ask them to read the directions carefully and to not discuss the test among themselves. When the participants turn the test over the directions say, "Please write your name and contact information in the blocks provided. DO NOT ANSWER ANY OF THE QUESTIONS BELOW OR WRITE ANYTHING ELSE ON THIS PAGE. Just wait five to ten minutes, and then turn the paper in as you leave." The trouble is, some people try to answer the questions, and when they do, they fail, regardless of whether or not their answer was right. Why? Because the Post Office wants people who follow directions and only do what is written.

As you can see, there are many, many ways to handle HR. The most important thing to remember throughout is: Prepare, remain calm, don't try to game the system, and be sure to thank everyone involved profusely upon leaving.

Sample Script: Your Greatest Strength

HR Director (looking down at your résumé in an attempt to appear nonchalant): "So, what do you think is your greatest weakness?"

You (after waiting until he or she looks back up at you): "I'd have to say my greatest weakness is I sometimes just don't know when to give up. When I identify an opportunity, I'm like a dog with a bone. This is why I like working with a team. Feedback helps me maintain my perspective."

HR Director: "That's great. Can you give me another example?"

You: "Well, speaking of teamwork, sometimes my energy can be a bit intimidating to people without my horsepower. I'm a fast thinker and speaker and I've learned I need to hold back sometimes—be more patient with the process. Since noticing this I've made a point of soliciting the opinions of the rest of the group before I move on to the next idea."

Presenting Your (Checkered) Past

It's not uncommon to have spent a few years cobbling together a professional life while juggling family commitments, or taking a few tries to find a work situation in which we feel we can thrive. The tricky bit is to know how to present these situations to a potential employer in such a way that you don't sound like you'll be out the door just after they get you acclimated. Here's what I would recommend:

If you're in the mood to get it over with, and your interviewer begins with "Where shall we start?" you could respond, "Well, if I were sitting where you're sitting I'd be concerned about the gaps in my résumé, so why don't we tackle that first."

It's always better to be on offense than defense.

If you want to hold off until things warm up a bit, you can wait for your interviewer to bring it up, at which point you can say, "I'm glad you asked me that."

In both cases, your segue is to "As you can imagine, single parenthood/caring for an aging parent necessitated a great deal of time and attention. That said, my children are older now/my father's routine is stabilized, so those factors are no longer in play."

If you've held a number of jobs because you had trouble settling on a career—or settling into the idea of working at all—you're going to need a slightly different response. In this instance, I would say, "As you can see, I've had the opportunity to try a number of different kinds of jobs, and I've learned a great deal from all of them—each provided skills that I was able to incorporate moving forward." I would then list the *very specific* reasons that brought you to this company. For example, "The reason I'm here today, however, is because I'm such a fan of your products/your values/your history."

In both scenarios, I would close with "This is a job to which I'm ready and willing to give a hundred percent."

The Compensation Conversation

Another question people struggle with is, "What's your current compensation?" and I agree this is a tricky one. Very few people are making what they want (or need) to earn, and they don't want to lowball themselves by talking about that number. They also recognize they must not fib. (Ever.)

So, what to do?

My recommendation is to pull a "debating politician" strategy. In other words, answer the question that you want to answer first.

Q: "What's your current compensation?"
A. "Well, I'm looking for a position that offers compensation in the range of $225K—more than I'm making right now, but also more in line with what I think I have to offer at this point in my career."

If they keep pushing: "My current compensation is lower than I'd like, which is part of why I'm looking for a new role."

And if they still keep pushing, it's possible you don't want to work for a boss who can't read cues. But if you do want to work for him, tell the truth. Lying is unacceptable and continued evasiveness will make you seem untrustworthy.

20 | The Artful Dodge

On a recent trip to Los Angeles, I ran into an acquaintance who greeted me effusively: "How are you? What are you doing here? How long are you here? We *have* to get together." When I told her I'd be there for two weeks, she looked a bit taken aback. Her follow-up? "It doesn't have to be this trip. . . ."

Ouch—and that ouch is for her. Because while there are many ways to dodge, or cancel, an invitation or commitment without offending, this isn't one of them.

What are some other mysterious/hilarious choices I've run into? Everything from a silk-lined "problem," such as, "I just *can't* cancel on my masseuse again," to a self-created "crisis" along the lines of "I've already committed to two parties that night."

And, of course, there's always the adult equivalent of "the dog ate my homework": "I didn't get your email."

Here's the thing: In every case, as in every moment, of your life, I want you to begin thinking of your word as your bond—as being as valuable as currency. And in the same way that you don't want to become known for writing checks that others can't cash, you don't want to get a reputation for accepting, or offering, invitations (or making commitments) on which you have no intention of following through.

"Okay," you may be thinking, "but everyone else does it. Is it really so terrible?"

No, it's not so terrible if you want to be like everyone else. This book, however, is for those who want to set themselves apart.

That said, I concede there are times when you find yourself look-

ing for a graceful way to extricate yourself from unwelcome commitments. With this in mind, here are a few responses to inconvenient
invitations and/or requests for your participation:

- "What a kind invitation—thank you. Unfortunately, I have
  plans for that evening."

- "Family commitments have me locked in for the foreseeable
  future. I'm sure you know how that goes. How's your family
  these days?"

- "You're so thoughtful to think of including me, but I wouldn't be
  able to give you a hundred percent. My current commitments
  have to be my focus. "

- "I'm afraid it's not something I can take on, but I appreciate
  your asking."

One consistent element I hope you noticed in the above is that
none includes the possibility that the situation will change. There's
nothing along the lines of "But I'll keep you posted" or "Now's not a
good time, but . . . ," both of which verbal tics are likely to end with
you having to repeat the conversation sooner rather than later.

Next, I'd like to address those people who issue invitations on
which they have no intention of following up. For example, the
chronic senders of emails that say, "We must get together! When are
you free?" To which—after you send dates and times—you never receive a response. I'm here to tell you to stop doing it. You gain no
goodwill. In fact, you lose credibility. (I'd also like to take a moment
to ask those of you who are chronic cancellers to take the time to organize yourself, and your calendar, properly. Don't make dates you
have no intention of keeping. Your time is no more important than
anyone else's. Short of sudden illness, accidents, or what insurance
policies refer to as "acts of God," twenty-four hours should be your

minimum cancellation policy. The French king Louis XVIII said, "*L'exactitude est la politesse des rois*": "Punctuality is the politeness of kings." Make it yours, too.

In today's world the value of currencies fluctuates day to day—a situation over which we have little control. Your good word, however, is something only you can devalue, so be courteous, be well calibrated, and, whenever possible, be kind.

The Toddler Treatment

For reasons passing my understanding (although I have some guesses . . . ahem, reality shows), it's somehow become acceptable to ask people about everything from how much they paid for their coat/car/house, to the intimacies of their GI tract, to the amount of their credit card debt. Alternatively, unsolicited opinions are offered, which require no less verbal finesse.

In every case, remember that the same rules that apply to handling toddlers intent on testing you will stand you in good stead here, since the reasons behind their questions are usually much the same—they just want to see what will happen. So: The shorter your answer the better off the situation is likely to end; keeping your sense of humor is critical; and, finally, consider the intention of those doing the asking—Are they bored? Malicious? Well intentioned? A known frenemy? A 200-horsepower social blunder?—and calibrate accordingly, because in the same way kids will drop it when they see they can't get a rise out of you, inappropriate questioners will also vanish once they realize you're not willing to play.

Problem Solving Is Personal

As noted in *How to Wow*, email is not for problem-solving. While it seems absurd that I need to expand on that, I've discovered I also need to note that neither text-messaging nor IMing is appropriate either (as one of my clients found out when she got a text announcing a deal was off—a deal with a signed contract, no less).

If you have to give someone bad news, if you're having a misunderstanding, if you feel a disagreement beginning to gather steam, pick up the phone, or go find the person. I don't care how uncomfortable you are. Taking immediate steps to put a human voice and/or face on the situation is going to lower the temperature immediately, which will ensure you remain uncomfortable for far less time.

Once you have the person in question available—and as hard as this may be—I recommend taking the initiative by beginning with what aspects of the misunderstanding you think you are accountable for. What I've discovered is that this is a fast way to help the other person take responsibility as well. Should you be confronted by someone who merely says, "Thanks," after which he or she continues to put forward their point of view, you're going to need to be prepared to listen to and acknowledge it. Once they've talked themselves out, you can say, "I know we both feel strongly about resolving this as easily and quickly as possible. What do you recommend we do to find a solution?"

In these moments, the use of "we," combined with your physical access, adds a human element to an abstract situation, guaranteeing as swift a resolution as possible.

21 | "You Can Discover More About a Person in an Hour of Play Than in a Year of Conversation"

Surprisingly enough, this quote comes from Plato. As we are discovering, and as he knew, people wear different masks at different times and in different places, and creativity and cooperation are sometimes best fostered in an atmosphere of fun (as evidenced by the widespread adoption of corporate "away days" and late-night "pizza sessions").

Tim Smit, the CEO of the innovative and wildly successful Eden Project (the world's largest greenhouse complex—including a 3.9-acre indoor rain forest), is the master of this approach. He has even codified it as "monkey business."

What does this mean? Well, Smit requires his Eden Project employees to prepare a meal for twenty of their coworkers once a year, resulting in a round of dinner parties which ensures that employees have ample time to see one another outside the standard work environment. (NB: The etymology of "companion" is "with bread"—you bond with those with whom you eat.)

Aside from the conviviality this fosters, Smit claims it's vital because important decisions shouldn't be made in the daytime. "Outside our nine-to-five existence, we change personality a little bit. In the dark, over a meal, blessed by wine—that's when the best instinctive decisions are made. That's when an organization makes the best ones too."

Smit also requires—in keeping with the Renaissance attitude I advocate here—that employees read a book they wouldn't otherwise have thought of reading and tell the others about it. They must do the same with a foreign film.

"That's all well and good," you may be thinking, "but when my workday's over the last thing I want to do is spend more time with the people from my office—particularly in situations where I might have to play 'trust games' or see them in shorts or bathing suits."

I couldn't agree more.

That said, this isn't about what you want to do. It's about what you need to do to achieve the best results possible for your team, your project, your organization—and yourself. And since this "monkey business" works, you need to find a way to make it work for you.

What, then, do I recommend?

Well, if, for example, you have been horrified the last few years over having to attend the company picnic and so have shown up late or not at all, why not speak with those involved in planning the event about, perhaps, changing it so it includes the possibility of bringing family or friends—thereby giving yourself additional time with your kids or spouse. Alternatively, with numerous charities and nonprofit organizations seeking ever-shrinking donations of time and money, why not organize the picnic as a fund-raiser or group activity for a local group that's in need? Either option is likely to make the day more palatable.

Another situation in which you're guaranteed to find that a spirit of play is helpful is when you're networking—where too often information-gathering ends up feeling like organ donation. How would I recommend you do this? If you're in charge of organizing an event, it can be very helpful to have it in an unconventional space— such as the local museum or a nearby exclusive hotel—and arrange with its staff for a brief discussion of the current exhibit or a tour of the amenities. Giving people a chance to focus on an activity or in-terest outside themselves will naturally spark non-work-related con-versations. Alternatively, you can arrange an evening with a business that's willing to share its expertise: a wine or cheese store that's willing to do tastings, a florist who will demonstrate arrangements, a sports store that can bring in the local pro to talk backhands or putts. Speaking from my own experience, one of the best networking events I ever put together revolved around learning how custom fragrances are "built" to convey a brand's identity. My friend Greg is still getting compliments for a networking paintball event he dreamed up.

If you are simply attending the event, it's no less important to be lighthearted. Yes, making connections is critical, but you'll get further if you approach others with questions about their kids or their hobbies before getting into their curriculum vitae or their EBITDA. And while you may not necessarily be riveted by how much they can bench-press, their child's conversation with the tooth fairy, or the ups and downs of their kitchen renovation, you will be making the kind of human connections that foster trust and encourage ongoing interaction: two highly sought-after networking outcomes.

Get Something on the Calendar

Should you be in the lucky position of having job security, please don't think you are off the hook with regard to networking. Keeping up with people when you don't have your back to the wall is no less important than when you do—and far easier on you both, because you won't be stressed and they won't feel obligated or overwhelmed. With this in mind, then, my request is that you schedule *at least* two meetings a month with people you've been meaning to get together with, or have wanted to meet. To keep it from feeling forced, fake, or in any way peculiar, mention a specific idea, plan, or project that you want to discuss with them when you make the call. And please do not use the phrase "pick your brain" when you do. It was always disgusting and now—even worse—it's overused.

Your Problems Are Not (Necessarily) Their Problems

As you come to know people better, it can be easy to think that you're friends as well as colleagues—and there are times this will be true.

That said, this is a fine line, and my general recommendation is: When in doubt, err on the side of formality.

For example, you may have a client with whom you've worked for some time and to whom you feel close. Consequently, when you're called for jury duty, you may say to him, "Hey, do you mind moving our meeting to X restaurant? I've got to be downtown all day."

The trouble is, he's your client and he's uptown. Your messy schedule isn't his problem, and it shouldn't become his problem. In fact, you stand a very good chance of pissing him off by making it his problem—no matter how chummy you've become over the course of working together.

Far better to call and ask to reschedule due to your conflict, then let him offer to change his plans should he be feeling friendly.

22 | You Must Have the Cattle

It's possible you've heard the metaphor "That guy is all hat and no cattle" to describe a person who overpromises and underdelivers, but I'm hoping you haven't. I'm also hoping that the fact that it isn't a phrase you hear day to day made it catch your attention, because in these days of ever-increasing information and ever-shortening attention spans, getting—and maintaining—people's attention and interest has become increasingly difficult. But it's also never been more important.

How to Wow recommended you begin keeping a quote file for use when you want to make a point, bolster an argument, or close with grace. This next idea is one I thought I'd throw out on the stoop to see if the cat licks it up (okay, you might not have liked reading that, but I'm willing to bet it caught your attention—which is my point): Begin an analogy and metaphor file, as both are effective ways to get, and keep, the attention of those around you.

But before I begin, I thought I'd take a moment to look at the difference between analogies and metaphors:

An analogy draws your attention to a similarity between like features of two things, on which a comparison may be based. For example, if you are in a business meeting where every aspect of the operation isn't under your control, but one surely is, you might say, "We can't choose our course, but we can choose the jockey." Another favorite, for use when those around you seem to be stuck in their thinking or planning, is "The only difference between a rut and a grave is the dimensions." Other pithy go-tos include "This is not the ditch to die in," for use when people are having trouble seeing the big picture, and "Spare me the labor pains—show me the baby," when someone's gotten himself bogged down in an enormous amount of extraneous detail. "Predicting rain doesn't count; building arks does" is useful when those around you are focused solely on the dire elements of a situation, and "You can't really tell who's skinny-dipping until the tide goes out" is a terrific replacement for the tired "Monday-morning quarterbacking."

A metaphor, on the other hand, is a figure of speech in which a term or phrase is applied to something to which it is not literally applicable in order to suggest a resemblance. My dictionary offered me, "A mighty fortress is our God." While I considered contributing, "I'm off like a prom dress," for your use in moments of leave-taking, I decided instead on, "Well, that went over like a lead balloon," although I sincerely hope this doesn't.

As you can see, incorporating both analogy and metaphor, or either, is a likely way to have people repeating your ideas when they leave the room.

Two other figures of speech I recommend collecting are aphorisms and epigrams. An aphorism is defined as "a terse saying embodying a general truth or astute observation," as can be seen in Benjamin Franklin's "In this world, nothing is certain but death and taxes." (A great place to look for these is www.aphorisms-galore.info.) An epigram is any witty, ingenious, or pointed saying tersely expressed, as in Oscar Wilde's "My own business bores me to death. I prefer other people's." (For more, see www.thehypertexts.com and search "epigrams.") Having a few of these in hand is useful when you're looking for a way to open your speech, headline your newsletter, or close your presentation.

Finally, a note about idioms, and the importance of learning the local vernacular:

An idiom is an expression whose meaning is not predictable when you break down its parts but that works as a whole, such as "Over my dead body," or "He's barking up the wrong tree." Idiom is also defined as a style of speech or phrasing that's indicative of a

particular place, business, or time. This idea is particularly important to keep in mind when you begin any new venture, as an ability
to adopt the local idiom goes a long way toward helping others feel
comfortable with you. For example, telling the owner of the bike
store that his excuse as to why the bicycle I'd ordered hadn't arrived
"lacked verisimilitude" probably added another month to my already
extended wait. On the other hand, although I know little to nothing
about sports, I discovered that bankers often use sports as a way to talk
about business. (One of my favorite moments in a tense meeting was
hearing, "Okay, so if we get that question, Lance, you quarterback it,
then everyone else pile on.") Given this, I made a point of learning
some sports terms I could toss around in those situations.

To succeed in your communication, sometimes you want to
stand out and sometimes you want to fit in—so listen carefully, decide which will get you further, and keep memorable options at the
ready.

Now You're Speaking My Language

As you begin researching job postings in your area of expertise, it's
important to reassure future employers that you are already "speaking
their language," as this makes it easier for them to imagine you fitting
smoothly into their culture—and simply polishing up your old résumé
isn't likely to give you the up-to-the-minute language being used to
describe recent occurrences and advancements in the field.

Given this, I recommend doing an in-depth check into how job
postings in this arena are being languaged. (A great place to look at
numerous job postings in your field is on theladders.com, a site that
lists jobs paying over $100,000 a year.)

What you might discover is that while the basic elements of the job
haven't changed, the way people are talking about those elements has.

For example, perhaps you were a consultant working with teams on
change management and you used to describe your work as "business
process redesign," but online research reveals that that's gotten a bad

name due to layoffs, and is now referred to as "business transformation." That small update to your résumé reassures HR professionals you're up to speed on news in the industry. Alternatively, perhaps your former job description was "Managed market research plans" but reading current job postings gives you language such as "Ran focus groups that uncovered consumer trends—providing sales team with the necessary information for fact-based selling." That's language that's going to make employers want to get in touch.

The Ten Worst Business Sayings

In addition to making your own language more colorful, I recommend noting the international research agency YouGov's study of the ten worst business sayings—any and all of which you might consider eradicating from your lexicon:

1. Thinking outside of the box
2. Touch base
3. At the end of the day
4. Going forward
5. All of it
6. Blue-sky thinking
7. Out of the box
8. Credit crunch
9. Heads-up
10. Singing from the same hymn sheet

To this I would add the following from my personal hit list of things I'd prefer not to hear my clients say:

1. Pick your brain
2. Drill down
3. Throw it against the wall and see what sticks

4. At this moment in time
5. 24/7
6. I, personally
7. The ball's in your court
8. It's not rocket science

It really isn't. . . . Most word-processing programs have a setting to check for clichés and tautologies—you need to make sure that your prose avoids them too.

Summing It Up:

- These days interviews and sales calls take all kinds of forms—lunches and dinners, theater trips and tennis games—and there are numerous ways, large and small, of knocking yourself out of the running. Do as much advance preparation as possible, and when in doubt, follow the lead of those around you.

- You're not "good": Awareness of this—and of other grammatical missteps—can reassure others you are their go-to person when they can't attend the meeting, the event, the conference.

- Incorporating the Six Layers of Why can lead to unexpected answers or insights, and ensures you won't fall back on useless modifiers when selling yourself or your product. (It's only great/amazing/incredible if you tell me *why*.)

- Close down any email accounts you may have with suggestive, cute, silly, or personal monikers or obscure combinations of letters and numbers. Buy your name as a URL, and set up an account with "your name@your name.com." Professionalism is paramount.

- Don't undermine your message with folksy, cutesy, or otherwise distracting salutations and closings. When in doubt, err on the side of formality, follow the lead of your superiors, or pick up a reference guide that can point you in the appropriate direction.

- Having the answers to frequently asked questions about you, your product, or your organization ensures that your message is consistent across the board, your staff is confident tackling anything they're asked, and your customer is getting the most in-depth, reliable information possible.

- There is an art to both remaining silent and interrupting. Silence is powerful when persuading, selling, and negotiating; knowing how to handle being interrupted, and how to gracefully interrupt others, is vital to your own, and others', personal and professional equanimity.

- Although the rituals of HR departments can seem byzantine, there is a system. Make the lives of their staffs easier by setting up and naming your résumé clearly. Make your own easier by knowing the answer to both your first and second "greatest strength/weakness" question, and prepping for case interviews in multiple formats.

- Your word is your bond. Don't commit to obligations on which you have no intention of following through. Should you want or need to pass on an event or commitment, ensure that your strategy is graceful.

- Studies have shown that creativity and cooperation are sometimes best fostered away from the workplace. With this in mind, build in time for your team to blow off steam as a group outside the office setting. Networking can also be more effective when it includes an activity in which everyone can participate.

- Keeping an analogy and metaphor file is useful, as incorporating these in your speech and writing are effective ways to get—and keep—the attention of those around you.

SECTION THREE
DO

Having acquired the habits and knowledge necessary to move forward with confidence and flair, it's now time to: "just" do it—the hardest thing of all.

(Suffice to say, I'm quite certain Nike is happy to have tied its profits to shoes sold, as opposed to miles run.)

Sections One and Two were designed to guarantee changes that are largely internal and personal. In order to impact on your situation, you must now take these changes out into the world because—properly handled—each and every one of the hundreds of one-on-one encounters you have every day is an opportunity to fine tune your "soft skills," gather information, and begin developing the comprehensive database necessary to succeed in today's business world.

Now, I do understand that test-driving new concepts can be hard. Sometimes it's because our perfectionism is so great that we don't want to risk doing something unless we know we're doing it "right." Sometimes it's because creative procrastination disguised as self-improvement has become a way of life: We're just going to take one more class and then we'll feel qualified. Sometimes it's because we've convinced ourselves that managing the crises of our loved ones is more important than keeping the focus on ourselves: Can't you see how brilliant s/he is? I need to support that.

Perhaps. But from where I sit, nothing can compare with the drama of you exploring your full potential as a human being.

Having had personal experience with almost all these roadblocks, I have made Section Three intensely practical, because—as noted—I've found that breaking large tasks down into discrete, tangible steps is the fastest way to see results. Information on how to organize or supersize your job search is offered, as is the technological ammunition you need to stay current outside your comfort zone— guaranteeing you'll always be steps ahead of your career peers. Concrete steps are given for how to accomplish the seemingly abstract task of maximizing others' trust, and insights into how to work the system—both in person and on the page—are offered, as are tools for going around the system, be it human or electronic. Finally, energizing your base by leveraging the power of favors, bartering your experience and intelligence, and building your personal advisory board is discussed.

My intention is for you to finish this section fired with genuine impatience to take the habits, knowledge, and skills you've learned out into the world, and to begin making the immediate changes necessary to bring your best self to the business of your life.

23 | Plan for Courage

One thing I've heard—and seen—over and over from clients the last few months is the debilitating effect of long-term stress and fear on their mental and physical health. Daily plunges in the stock market, daily announcements of layoffs, and nonstop doomsday commentary by the media left many of them feeling so overwhelmed they literally were incapable of deciding what to do next. And in the middle of all this, they were having to put on a brave face for family and friends, and keep an upbeat attitude at the office, which drained their resources still further. By the time I was called in, a number of them were in a state of near collapse. They weren't returning calls. They were canceling appointments. They weren't sleeping a lot—or they were, but in the middle of the day.

Why was my expertise needed? Because over the years that I've been teaching people to present themselves I've learned that in the same way stuffing down nervousness only makes you more nervous, stuffing down your anxiety and fear only makes you more anxious and fearful. When you're getting ready to speak in public, you have to embrace your nervousness—work with it to give you the energy and commitment you need to carry your audience with you. The same is true for handling anxiety or fear. These emotions are appropriate responses to stressful situations. The fact that you're feeling them isn't a problem—what's important is that you recognize and handle them. And in fact, a critical component of courage is recognizing it is *not* fearlessness. Instead, it is the quality that allows you to do what needs to be done in the face of fear—both yours and other people's.

Are there specific things you can do to help make courage an easier choice? There are. In fact, one of the most seemingly mundane things you can do is to start keeping checklists. That's right, checklists: those workaday items that inevitably get left on the front of the refrigerator when you leave for the supermarket. But before you skip ahead, thinking this is too simple to be an effective tool for you, consider that both surgeons and pilots must complete rigorous checklists before they begin operations. Pilots have a list of more than twenty-five items that must be checked off, in order, every time they leave the ground, despite the fact that most of them know the list by heart, and December 2007's *New Yorker* contained an extraordinary article about a one-man crusade over the past seven years to make intensive-care units safer in our country. The work of this man, Peter Pronovost, has already, in the words of the article, *"saved more lives than that of any laboratory scientist of the last decade."* How did he do it? By instituting checklists.

If you're still feeling skeptical, consider the Marine Corps phrase, "Checklists are written in blood": another world in which mistakes can have grave consequences.

So, what kind of checklists am I talking about? Well, if you have a big meeting coming up that's making you nervous, you might consider instituting a presentation checklist that includes:

1. Have I identified what I want my audience's primary takeaway to be?

2. Do I know my opening story, and my closing thought?

3. Do I know the cues and the choreography—whom I follow, and who follows me? If I am being introduced by someone else, have we discussed what he or she will say? If I am introducing myself, do I know what I'm going to say? If I'm passing the baton to the person behind me, have I spoken with him about what he would like me to say?

4. If this is a presentation that I give regularly, have I checked that my slides do not contain references to the previous engagement?

5. Have I done an advance recon on the room to check the lighting, the sound quality, the podium, the microphone? Am I *sure* I have the right cable to connect my computer to the system?

6. In keeping with that idea, if others are in charge of the technical aspects of the day, have I introduced myself to them, and do I have their cellphone number? There are very few people you want more on your side than the ladies and gentlemen in charge of audiovisual.

7. Do I know the names, titles, and background of every person who will be attending? Have I built acknowledgment of their presence and thanks to the appropriate parties into my remarks?

8. Do I know the answers to the worst three questions I anticipate getting? Sometimes I like to preempt these by starting my Q&A session by asking them of myself. For example, "Some of you may be wondering how I could bring up X given our sales figures from the last quarter, but . . .," and then offering my best answer.

9. Have I thought about the timing of any handouts? Will the audience already have them, or will I need to distribute them? Should that be done before, while, or after I speak?

Speaking from my own experience, having a checklist of this kind has saved me from disaster on more than one occasion—and the confidence I've gained from ticking off each item beforehand has meant my mind was free to deal with the multiple factors over which I didn't have complete control.

What other practices might you implement to help institutional-ize courage? If you are dreading a conversation—with your boss about your performance review, with colleagues about their work habits, with your employees about a difficult decision—one way to plan for courage is to practice having the conversation out loud with someone whose judgment you trust. Yes, this will feel deeply uncomfortable at first— it's far too much like the "make-believe" games of your childhood—but it is only when you practice out loud that you hear the holes in your argument, can begin to consider the tone of your voice, and will be able to get feedback about how to manage your physicality. My recommendation is to first run it with you as yourself and your friend as the person (or people) in question. Then swap roles. This is incredibly helpful, as it allows you to hear how someone else might tackle the same situation. If there are specific phrases or ideas that come up that are useful, write them down in longhand. As was discussed in How to Wow, doing so will embed them in your body more deeply, making it far easier for you to remember them during your high-stakes moment.

Finally, if your fear is very specific, you might embark on a "confidence course" of doing small, not-too-scary things that allow you to build toward the bigger thing. For example, if you want to ask your boss about a raise, you might begin with a low-stakes activity like entering a store and asking for change for a dollar. Then you might graduate to negotiating with sellers at yard sales and flea markets. After that, you might give your phone or credit card company a call and see if you can talk your way into better rates. Finally, you might make a checklist of all the questions you anticipate having to answer in your meeting with your boss, role-play your answers with a friend, and get the appointment in your boss's calendar, knowing that you've planned for courage.

Ralph Waldo Emerson said, "Do the thing you fear and the death of fear is certain." Taking this approach to courage ensures that while you might not start looking forward to doing those things you fear, you will find yourself rising to the occasion despite that fear—my definition of courage.

There's a New Kid in Town

One of the side effects of our shifting economy is that people are moving to find work, or being transferred by the head office to a different branch of their company. As you know, studies put a move of this kind right behind death and divorce on the list of greatest stresses to the system. The following checklist is one way to offset the vertigo that can come from this type of rapid geographic change:

1. Take a bus tour of the city. (Do all touristy things right away.)
2. Subscribe, preferably in advance, to the local version of *Time Out* magazine. You may not be able to do everything, but at least you'll know what's happening.
3. Read the classified ads or the local Craig's List postings for a week—there's no better window on your new world.
4. Read the government/community section of the phone book. Usually these are an overlooked mine of information, and will have the answers that newcomers need (and that even established residents frequently don't know).
5. In the same vein, where is the nearest twenty-four-hour pharmacy, late-night diner, FedEx, and Kinkos?
6. If you're moving into a development or community with rules about everything from dogs to garbage sorting to the height of children's playhouses, find and read the rules carefully; it would be a pity to needlessly alienate your neighbors before you've even had the opportunity to meet them by breaking rules that you didn't know existed.
7. Spend fifteen minutes studying a map of the city. Use the information as described below.
8. Spend some time with an atlas to understand the city's geography and "microclimate." Frequently, a glance at the atlas explains why the city is there in the first place (like it's at the confluence of two rivers). Google Earth is, of course, great for this.
9. Read a history of the city and visit the local museum. Why are the

major streets called what they are called? Why is the city here instead of fifteen miles south? What are the "eras" of the city?

10. Learn the three largest local employers and try to tour one of them. Who owns them?

11. Even if you have no kids, learn about local schools, both reputation and schedule. Same for local universities. Education is too big a part of other people's lives for you to be completely unaware of, and other people moving to town are sure to ask you. (I had one client who considered his subordinate's vacation requests highly eccentric until he found out that the local school system did not break for summer, but did a six-weeks-on, two-weeks-off schedule.)

12. Learn state/city bird, flower, motto, etc. These little pieces of trivia help you understand more about the history and identity of the city or state, usually open up another avenue of its history, and help make much of what you see and hear make sense.

In a similar vein . . .

13. Even if you are not religious, learn the top three denominations, etc.

14. Bloomberg devotes part of its website to letting you set up and track local stocks. Do that for the area. Everyone else does.

15. Learn the sports teams (and coaches' names), local politicians' (and their spouses') names, etc.

16. Join a charity and a cultural organization (museum, symphony, etc.).

17. While you're there, look at the names on the donor wall. Do some research into those people whose names appear prominently.

18. At least be aware of the existence of major country and city clubs.

19. Keep a map of your neighborhood on your refrigerator and as you meet your neighbors, pencil in their names and any salient details: kids, dogs, etc.

As you can see, if you were to do even half of these things, you would feel far more at home, far more quickly—acclimation that would free you up to be fully mentally engaged in making your mark in your new business environment. Engaging your spouse and/or kids in some of the activities on this list is also a way to ease any feelings of rootlessness they might be experiencing.

"Can You Come Speak to an Old Friend?"

As those of you who've read *How to Wow* know, I was a mad, crazy fan of *The West Wing*. My point in bringing it up here is that there was a phrase everyone on the senior staff knew to use when they needed to pull someone out of a meeting or social situation gracefully in order to deal with something of utmost urgency, and that was "I was wondering if you could come speak to an old friend of the president's?"

How does this have relevance to you? Well, if you work in a situation in which you're surrounded by customers or clients whom you don't want to spook, it can be helpful to have a phrase of this kind in hand for getting someone to come with you immediately.

For instance, I was recently talking to a client who owns a restaurant. As I'm sure you know, going to a restaurant is about far more than the food you eat: It's also about the staff, the ambiance, the ease of the entire experience. Given this, I recommended that in moments when a member of his staff had to be pulled away from what she was doing, the phrase "Have you seen the Spanish wine list?" be used.

The beauty of this? Its innocuousness was guaranteed not to rouse the curiosity of any customer who might hear it and—because this was a French restaurant—there *was* no Spanish wine list.

Similar to the codes many married couples use to signal "Let's leave this party now," having a standardized "I need you now" phrase ensures that you and your staff have a graceful way to move from one situation to another.

"Let Us Not Commit Suicide for Fear of Death"

This quote from a German kaiser is a favorite—and one that's particularly important to remember when you're nervous about how you, your idea, or your organization is going to be received.

Too often, however, for any number of reasons—because we're concerned about being wrong, because a lower profile seems a safer bet, because taking chances in an uncertain economy seems too risky—we don't speak up in meetings, or we short-circuit our creative process, and failure becomes a self-fulfilling prophecy.

For example, in these days of cost-cutting, it's possible your CEO might come into a meeting with a freshly created business plan, to which he's visibly very attached. Unfortunately, you, and those around you, know that one of the tests he cut out of the production process is critical to ensuring its safety. The trouble is no one's saying anything. Their mind balloons are reading, "Well, he'll find out eventually—I'm not going to tell him." Speaking up in this moment—while it may initially earn you fire and brimstone—is more than likely to be rewarded in the long run, because while those around you will likely pipe up after the fact, you will be remembered as the one who had the courage to speak in the moment.

24 | Job Search Secret: "Do It, Delegate It, or Delete It"

This Marine Corps maxim is applied to any request that comes in—verbally, telephonically, or electronically. It's the idea behind touching each piece of paper only once.

This discipline is critical not only to instilling confidence in those around you, but to maintaining confidence in yourself. Why? Because the lurking knowledge that you're procrastinating is a confidence-killer. And in the same way that it's hard to feel at the top of your game when you know you've left behind piles of laundry, an unmade bed, and a sinkful of dirty dishes, it's hard to present your best self to the world knowing you have an in-box that's overflowing with requests, complaints, and exhortations.

For instance, let's say you're beginning your job interview process. Most of us start out methodically, and with purpose. Over time, however—as multiple leads come in, multiple résumés get written, and multiple phone calls are made—both our desk and our email in-box become filled with leads and questions, the neglect of which paralyzes our thinking and keeps us from moving forward with efficiency. Instituting a "Do It, Delegate It, or Delete It" mind-set enables you to follow up, and follow through, with greater efficiency.

For example, "Do" items include following through on all leads, from all sources—checking every company's or connection's background. While you may not end up posting résumés or picking up the phone to make a connection on every one of them, you need to keep the mind-set that right now, your job search *is* your job. Don't allow yourself to be sidetracked. What, specifically, are you looking for? Any information on a company's mission/bestselling product/competition, which can then help you position yourself as being able to contribute to furthering its goals, enhancing its status, or plugging the hole in its offerings via skill sets and ideas that are unique to you.

You might think doing this research is something you can delegate, but I've found this isn't the best use of delegation—a highly underrated skill set, by the way. It's far better to delegate those tasks that many of us use as a form of creative procrastination, disguised as "necessary" work: reformatting our résumé, updating our website, even getting our interview wardrobe ready—all of which give us a seemingly morally unimpeachable response to the question "What are you doing to further your search?" when, in fact, they are avoidance behaviors. Truly. Unless you are a designer or web developer, these tasks are generally best handed off to those trained in these skill sets. Not only will you give yourself the time you need to focus on what you alone can do, you'll likely end up with a far better-looking document or site.

I recommend deleting from your to-do list items along the lines of multiple postings of your résumé—and the consequent follow-up—on websites with "credentials" along the lines of "Lose 9 pounds of belly fat in one day." Focused follow-through on personal recommendations and with accredited sites (say, for example, www.monster.com or www.theladders.com) is far more likely to yield the results you seek. I also suggest deleting those leads you find via what I call "Internet daydreaming." This generally looks like a job that was something you considered doing during your summers off in high school and just happens to be available in Hawaii.

I do not, however, recommend deleting following up on any personal leads you are offered. While it may be tempting to delete from your to-do list following through on the suggestion you got from your child's camp counselor to get in touch with her cousin "because it seems like you have so much in common," following through could reveal this cousin is the vice president of the firm you've been angling for a connection to for the last six months. (But regardless of whether or not they result in the outcome you want, you need to remember that personal leads are just that—personal. Thanking the people who offer them is mandatory to building the kind of effective, comprehensive network you will always need.)

As you can see, while it may seem either strident or simplistic, adopting a "Do It, Delegate It, or Delete It" policy gives you a framework for following up and following through in such a way that your mind is free to give 100 percent of its focus to your day's priorities.

Abandon All Nonessential Functions

As many of you know, when your body is in distress, it shuts down all nonessential functions. (This is why fear so often causes our mouths to go dry: Salivation is, essentially, nonessential.)

Our bodies are infinitely wise.

If you are having trouble focusing on your job search, my recommendation would be to apply this same innate wisdom to the process: Take a long, hard look at what activities you currently consider essential and then consider whether or not they are, in fact. (I mean, I'm guessing that up until a few seconds ago you thought salivation was essential and *that's* on the list. . . . You really don't have anything that can go?) Ask yourself: Is it really necessary for me to have that lunch, or do I just feel like getting caught up with so-and-so? Do I really need to redesign my website *completely* before I send out my résumé, or is it sharp enough to focus instead on getting some résumés actually posted today? Do I really have to have my five-year plan complete before I go pitch my idea, or can I start making calls next week?

In short, are some of these just the job search version of "I can't go to the gym until I lose five pounds"?

Research Roundup

I've talked a lot about doing your background research on the company, and many of you may be thinking, "Well, that sounds great in theory, but what specifically am I looking for?" At minimum, I recommend always having answers to the following:

1. Why you want to work in the industry.

   This is an often-overlooked softball question. For example, if you're talking to Citibank, it's possible they will begin with "Why do you want to be in finance?" This question almost demands a story along the lines of "From the time I was X years old . . ." that includes a precipitating incident and concludes with "and I've been passionate about it ever since." This answer is particularly important if you are changing sectors (i.e., moving from garden design to retail fashion). You must have a reason beyond "I need a job"—even if that's true.

2. Why you want to work for that particular company.

   Here is where you speak to their mission, their corporate values, their vision, etc., and then position yourself as being able to contribute to furthering their goals, enhancing their status, or plugging the hole in their offerings via skill sets and ideas that are unique to you. How do their goals mesh with yours? As in a good cover letter, this is a chance to speak about *their* needs in terms of *your* abilities. (Cover letter side note: The basic opening theme of cover letters should be "My understanding is that your company needs X, Y, and Z"—i.e., open with what you know about *them* and what you believe are *their* needs. You can *then* move on to why you can meet those needs, "especially because this has been a lifelong goal," etc. . . . The point is, you want to open by talking about them and their requirements, and then show how well you match. Do this, and they'll be pleasantly surprised.)

3. What their bestselling product is and why.

If it is a consumer product, it would be great if you've actually tried it. At bare minimum, make sure that you're not wearing, carrying, driving, etc. the competition. One consultant I know who worked in the telecom industry was smart enough to keep three brands of cellphones in his briefcase. Before meetings, he would move SIM cards from phone to phone as appropriate. He'd started this practice when potential clients at Palm commented on the BlackBerry he was carrying. One MBA student I know borrowed a friend's Ford to attend his interview there. When he got the job, he sold his Toyota before reporting for work!

4. Who their competition is, and why.

If they are not a consumer brand, or you are new to the industry and aren't quite sure, Hoover's (www.hoovers.com) is a big help in this, as are stock reports on the company or industry, which are made available by brokerages like Charles Schwab (www.charlesschwab.com). What I've discovered is that even if the company I am interested in is not publicly traded, the broker will have reports that explain in layman's terms the big players in an industry, how the companies in it have been doing lately, all the latest important news about the business, etc. And unlike looking at whatever Google throws up that day, you can also be sure that this industry information has been sorted through for relevance and (relative) evenhandedness.

5. How many employees/offices they have (and the locations of their offices).
6. Any and all subsidiary brands.
7. Any industry infighting.

This last one can be tough and is often overlooked even by the best of us. (As those of you know who remember when Tiger Woods thanked Arthur Andersen—as opposed to Andersen Consulting—for sponsoring a golf tournament when he was on Andersen Consulting's payroll; partners of each were in the audience, and the two firms were in the midst of a bitter corporate divorce.) That said, they don't call it the World Wide Web for nothing—do take the time to check beyond the first five entries Google throws up. (If nothing turns up by entry twenty, however, you've likely done your due diligence.)

8.   Your interviewer's background.

While you don't want to walk in with a creepy level of detail, you should know where she went to school, how long she's been with the company, etc. Questions about her experience with the company—what does she like best about the corporate culture, etc.—are also a nice thing to ask should she inquire, "Do you have any questions for me?" ("Do you have any questions for me?" is also a good time to ask about her company's plans for growth over the next five years.)

9.   The general salary range for that position within the industry.

You won't want to bring up a number unless interviewers do—but should they ask what your proposed salary might be, you want to be able to give them a range that's in the industry ballpark.

Job Interview Time Line

Once you've got the job interview, it can suddenly feel like there are any number of things you need to tackle immediately. In order to help my clients prioritize—and keep from becoming overwhelmed—I put together the following job interview time line:

72 Hours Before:

- Start your research. As noted, this is something you need to do yourself.

- Decide on what you will be wearing and take anything that needs to be cleaned to the dry cleaner.

48 Hours Before:

- Put together your list of potential questions and answers and practice out loud. If at all possible, have someone you trust videotape your Q&A, watch it with you, and offer constructive feedback.
- I've said it before, but it bears repeating: Make sure that you have a work-relevant, crisp response to that softball interview opener "So, tell me about yourself. . . ."

24 Hours Before:

- Pick up the dry cleaning you took in two days ago.
- Check the weather report and make any necessary changes or additions to your wardrobe depending on what you discover: umbrella, different shoes or jacket, etc.
- MapQuest your route or program your GPS: It's not enough to have a general idea of where you're headed.
- Know where you are planning to park, and how long it will take to get from there to your interview. Many big companies have multiple entrances. HR departments are pretty good about specifying these, but be sure you know the one to which you're headed. On some corporate "campuses" there is even an internal shuttle bus for you to catch once you are on their grounds. (I have seen this at both software and pharmaceutical companies.) Again, HR is usually pretty good about preparing you for this, but it's important to be mentally prepared.
- Print out two copies of your résumé: one for you and one for your interviewer. I can't tell you how often I've heard stories of interviewers not having a client's résumé in front of them. Having two gives you the opportunity to help them look better when they're shuffling through the papers on their desk saying, "I know I had it right here. . . ." (That said, don't make a big deal of handing it over. An easy "Oh, I brought an extra" is perfect.)

- Polish your shoes. If you have Edge Dressing or Scuff Cover—two truly miraculous shoe-maintenance products—be sure to detail the edges. This is what the professionals do.
- Polish your briefcase or portfolio and make sure it is loaded with a pad, the aforementioned two résumés, and two pens. One big caution: Buff your briefcase or portfolio carefully when you're finished—the last thing you need is black polish from your lovely-looking portfolio ending up on your slightly sweating palms, freshly laundered shirt or trousers, etc.
- If you're a smoker, you might consider getting a nicotine patch (not gum) to help with your nerves that day.

Day of:

- Don't brush your teeth in your interview outfit. (Do brush them, however.) The last thing you need is a big blob of toothpaste, or a water stain, on your freshly ironed shirt.
- Double-check that you have picture ID with you in case you have to identify yourself to security.

15 minutes before:

- Be outside the building. If you do want or need something to eat or drink, please don't choose something that might stain (coffee, tea, etc.) or explode. (Yes, I saw that happen with a jelly doughnut.)

10 minutes before:

- Be in the lobby. This will give you time to clear security if necessary, wander into the wrong elevator bank and correct your course, stop on multiple floors if you happen to be coming in at the beginning or middle of the day, etc.
- If there is a parking ticket to validate, get this done now. You don't want to have to come back in sheepishly after a triumphant exit. In

any case, never ask the executive or the HR people to do this for you if you can avoid it.

5 Minutes Before:

- Be in front of the receptionist. Please be sure to greet this person courteously on both your way in and your way out of the building. Remember, he or she will likely be polled as to what they thought of you.

25 | Have a Thick Face

As you know, in many Asian cultures, including China, "face"—reputation, dignity, or prestige—is important both in business and in daily life, and a great deal of time is spent ensuring not only that you don't lose face, but that you never cause another to do so.

What many people don't realize is that as a practical matter some people's "faces" are "thicker" than others—in other words, instead of being governed by exquisite rules of honor, etiquette, and behavior in every situation, many Chinese people are tough and flexible, yet still retain "face." That mode of being is called having a "Thick Face."

There is, however, another definition of having a "Thick Face" that was introduced to me by a gentleman who had been working in China for many years. His story began when he and his company were invited to bid to undertake a major infrastructure project near Xian, a prospect about which they were very excited. They were less excited when they learned that all their competitors had also received similarly effusive invitations to bid. When my friend asked a more experienced comprador what was going on, he was told, "The mayor has a Thick Face—he does this all the time. Either he has a nephew working for a competitor who wants to learn all he can about your sector and the various offerings, or he just wants to give his sons some negotiation practice. He probably has no intention of buying anything from any of you, but he won't lose face when negotiations mysteriously collapse—he's happy to put you to work for his own ends, even if it wastes your time." As you can see, this definition of a Thick

Face implies something more—a certain shrewdness, even ruthlessness, in dealing with outsiders.

How can this notion be helpful to you? After all, many people would regard these as hardball or "unfair" techniques, and there are certainly situations in which I would agree. That said, there is value to this idea within the realm of job interviews—in particular, going on interviews despite the fact that you have no intention of taking the job. What's the point of the exercise, then? After all, your friends will think you've been on tons of interviews and never been hired, a situation that might cause you to feel you've lost face. If you adopt a Thick Face, however, you won't mind that downside, because you're getting interview and negotiation practice—an exercise that's never wasted.

For example, if you're working on your responses to your greatest strength/weakness, now is the time to see which answers garner the best reaction. If you've found you choke when asked, "So, what kind of number are you looking for?" now is the time to name a number at the high end of outrageous, just for the practice of doing so with equanimity. If there is a hole in your résumé or skill set that always makes you flinch, now is your opportunity to practice discussing it with candor and ease.

And finally, there's always the possibility you'll go on an interview for a job you never thought you'd want and find out it's exactly what you're looking for.

Just Say Yes

Every now and then an unexpected phone call is good news: In this case, you're asked to come in for an impromptu interview. In these moments, it's possible you might not be in a job-hunting frame of mind, and so your answer to "Can you come in today at three?" might sound something like "Hang on. I need to check with my babysitter/my partner/my trainer." This is not good. In these moments, the only answer to the question is "Yes." After that, hang up and figure out the details on your own time. Similarly, if inquiries are made about a skill set that can be acquired via a weekend's worth of hard work on your part—for example, "Do you know how to run a focus group? Embed video in a Keynote presentation? Coordinate a marketing newsletter e-blast?" even if in the moment you have *no idea* how you might do such a thing, your answer should be "Yes." After that, cancel your plans and do the research.

Sample Script: Embed Yourself

Interviewer: "So, do you know how to embed a video in a Keynote presentation?"

You (internal dialogue): "What?? Is that even possible??"

 (external dialogue): "That isn't something that's required at my job—which has been an ongoing frustration for me, since it's a valuable skill to have. What I've done to address that is research it on my own time. If you feel it's critical for me to know, I'll have it mastered by my start date."

Be "Dress-Ready"

What else can you do to prepare for an impromptu interview request? The Marine Corps recommends keeping a "dress-ready" uniform in one's kit at all times. I recommend you have an interview-ready suit in your closet at all times, plus up-to-the-minute business cards, résumé, and/or portfolio. This means you can spend the time between the phone call and your interview refreshing your mind on the details of the company in question, not running to the dry cleaner or copy shop. Once you've got the job, *always* travel with an extra white shirt and tie (or their female equivalents) on business trips. In fact, many professionals leave a complete change of business clothes at the office for their assistants to courier or FedEx them at a moment's notice. If you haven't got that luxury, the trunk of your car isn't a bad place for this "Professional's Emergency Kit."

26 | Do Go There

The phrase "Don't go there" has entered common usage, having become the shorthand way of telling people to abandon their current line of reasoning or questioning. I'm here to tell you that, more often than not, you should go there — in this case the "there" in question being the decision-maker in charge of your inquiry, your request, or your future.

For example, say you find a posting for your dream job on the Web. While it's important to post your résumé and information according to the guidelines presented, I would also recommend writing a note to the CEO/CFO/VP to whom you would ultimately report noting that you've done so, but also including the specifics of the value you plan to add to the company on your arrival, then dropping that note in the mail, or at the office itself. Please understand, however, that this just means dropping the note at the office. This does not mean attempting to get past the gatekeepers to plead your case. (I can't emphasize enough how important this is: Leaping out of the woodwork at people is incredibly off-putting.)

That said, physically putting yourself in the person's sight line can be a great thing to do, provided it's accomplished with finesse. As being good at outwitting callers like yourself is likely one of the many qualifications gatekeepers must have, it's far better to work on establishing camaraderie with them by introducing yourself, finding out their name, and asking their advice about the best way to move forward. The key word there is "advice." When they feel like you're attempting to circumnavigate them, they will block you on principle; when you defer to their experience/expertise and enlist their aid by giving them the "because" behind why you are making your request, they are much more likely to accede. (As was discussed in *How to Wow*, giving people the "because" increases the possibility of their cooperation from 60 to 94 percent.)

When you do ask their advice, I would put it in both the most proactive and the most low-stakes way imaginable: "I'm planning to be in your neighborhood/in town next week. Do you think there is five minutes at either the beginning or the end of any day that he would be able to see me? I wanted to ask you because . . ." Tacking it onto another trip you are ostensibly making to the area keeps you from seeming too much like a stalker. Putting a five-minute time limit on it demonstrates that you recognize this is an imposition. As noted, the "because" helps people feel they are part of the decision-making process.

Should you be rebuffed, you want to take it with good humor: "Of course. I just thought I'd suggest it. I'm in and out of your part of town quite a bit, however, so I may give you a call again in a week or so." When you do call back, remember, it's a fresh start: Yes, you know the gatekeeper's name, but what's been going on in his world? Find out. He has a rich and full life outside your phone calls. Making the time to get to know something about that helps strengthen your connection. Then explain you're again going to be in his neighborhood, give him the "because" behind why you'd like five minutes with his boss, and ask for a specific five minutes of the boss's time. Whether it's granted this time or not, I'd suggest writing the gatekeeper a thank-you note for his trouble. Because if he's still keeping you at bay, this is just the kind of personal touch that might have him put in a favorable word for you, which means the next call could be from his boss, looking for you. Once you've gotten the face-to-face time you've been seeking with the C-level executive—in addition to demonstrating all the ways you will add value to the firm once you've been hired—be sure to take a moment to acknowledge his assistant's value too.

Woody Allen claims that 80 percent of success is just showing up.

Taking the time to put yourself, either on paper or in person, in the sight line of the person pulling the trigger on the decision is one more way you can help to guarantee your success.

Bypass the Bureaucracy

We all know the frustration of listening to a prerecorded voice telling us to "Press or say 'one' for sales; press or say 'two' for technical support. . . ." Similarly, we've all had the experience of being told, "No, I'm afraid he's not available this week. May I take another message?"

Here are a few ways to bypass this bureaucracy:

If you are dealing with an automated system, regardless of the situation, the best choice to make if you want to speak to a human being is to press the button that mentions sales, as I guarantee they will have staffed the section that's in charge of taking your money. Once you have a person on the phone, introduce yourself and ask him his name. Then explain the situation you're trying to resolve and ask how he would suggest you move forward. When he says you need to call another number, request both that he perform the transfer and that he stay on the line until there is an actual third person on the phone.

If you are trying to resolve a situation via the Web, and have sent emails to the suggested customer service mailbox, to no avail, check around on the site for the contact information for a public relations or press office. At this point, I don't recommend sending an email, as that's too easy to ignore, but calling. Again, I guarantee this is one area of the company that will be staffed with living, breathing people, as maintaining its public image is likely a priority. Once you have someone on the phone, the same procedures apply: Introduce yourself, get his or her name, explain your situation, and ask how best to proceed.

27 | Call with No News

"I'm calling to tell you I have no news." This phrase, one I heard recently from my doctor, left me swooning—and not because he was calling to tell me about a benign diagnosis. What, then, was he calling about? *He was calling to tell me he had no news.*

Why was I so enraptured by this? Because he had said he would call . . . AND HE DID—even though, as noted, he had no news.

What I've discovered, and I'm sure you've noticed it too, is that people will say, "Oh, I'll call and let you know about thus and such" and then . . . silence. When you finally do hear from them—either because you could no longer stand the silence and called them, or because you find yourselves standing behind them in the "10 Items or Less" line—they explain that they didn't call because they never did get the answer to your question, or get access to the information you required. If you're like me, your internal monologue (or—let's call a spade a spade—rage-alogue) in these moments is "Well, why on earth didn't you call me and tell me *that*??"

Why is this important? It's important because we're all busy people. Getting a status report of this kind allows us either to move forward and attempt to gather the information elsewhere, or choose to remain in a holding pattern with this person. My point is, we are left feeling like we have a choice. We are able to retain the semblance of control.

But beyond that courtesy, it's important because operating in this way is critical to building others' trust—and trust is vital to credibility. If you become known as someone who takes the time to pick up the phone and follow through—regardless of the status of the job you are following through on—you are far more likely to be able to persuade people to give you time when you need it, a referral when you ask for it, and the deal because you deserve it.

There are, of course, exceptions to this rule: an entire theory of management calls for "reporting by exception." The idea—practiced de facto by many efficient people and organizations—is that leaders be spared from hearing about routine, planned, expected, or irrelevant information: reporting such matters just wastes their and their subordinates' time. Instead, reporting by exception calls for immediate feedback and reporting in the event of any extraordinary situation or circumstance out of the scope of the junior employees. The implicit rule is "No news is good news," and it works well in high-trust environments.

But be honest: Most of the time that you don't hear from people—or don't get back to them—it is not because you're a fanatic about reporting by exception. In my experience, in fact, people who *are* fanatical about it tend to explicitly state, "You'll only hear from me if there is a problem: No news is good news." If you plan on taking that approach, I recommend being this overt with regard to stating your follow-up policy.

For the rest of us, however, calling with no news is the better choice, as it's rare to be penalized for being too conscientious.

For example, perhaps you're talking with a group of people at a cocktail party and find yourself connecting well with someone whose background you don't know, but whose interests you appear to share. "I'll send you a link to an article I read," you might say. Now, in the normal course of things, it's possible your offer will exit your consciousness by the time you arrive home. Taking the time to follow through on your offer of information, however, might mean you end up sending your information to the vice president of a firm you've always admired. And now you've made a connection—a connection he's far more likely to remember because you weren't, technically, "networking" when it was made. You were, however, exhibiting just those qualities most prized by firms searching for talent: initiative, follow-through, and keeping one's word.

Sometimes the reason for our silence is because we know that the person on the other end of the line is sitting by his phone like a teenager waiting for a prom date—and we fear that telling him we have no news is going to be extremely disappointing to him. That said—as those of you who are job candidates know—there are few times more agonizing than waiting for a call to learn if you got a job. A Friday afternoon call to a candidate waiting for news to say that you have no news (but that, in effect, he's not forgotten) goes a long way toward granting the job seeker a relaxed weekend. For this reason, when I work with HR professionals, I am insistent they make those calls. There's another reason to make the call as well: It goes a long way toward inclining a candidate to accept their offer, if and when it is made, over that of a rival firm. In fact, I can think of very few techniques that make corporate vision statements about "valuing people" come alive more.

Another reason we often don't make the uncomfortable call is because we know that the fact that we currently have no news is likely to turn into the receiver's bad news. While these can be tough calls to make, they are the ones I particularly highly recommend, as the making of them—despite your discomfort—goes a long way toward forestalling a pyrotechnic blowout when you do, ultimately, have to call with the bad news. Here's an example from my own career:

When I was working in publishing, I signed a book with an agent who was a very big deal—one with not just an industry-wide but a worldwide reputation. We did the deal at the end of the November, and one of the key things stressed to me was that, for tax reasons, the author needed her signing check before the end of the calendar year. Unfortunately, halfway through the month of December, when I called to see how things in accounts payable were coming along, I discovered that our AP department—flooded with end-of-the-year requests and at half-staff due to the upcoming holidays—was unlikely to have this done for me. In that moment, it would have been very easy not to be in touch with my author's agent: to simply hope that accounts payable was going to be able to pull a rabbit out of its hat and leave well enough alone. Instead, I took a deep breath, called the agent, and told him that while I was going to move heaven and earth to make this happen, it was unlikely. While the conversation began stickily, I can tell you that it ended well—in fact, his exact words were "I respect the fact that you picked up the phone."

Did we ultimately get her the check? No. Did I, however, become one of his favorite people to submit book proposals to? I did.

So despite the circumstances that make it easier to forget or avoid the call—because it was just a "conversational drive-by," or because you don't want to disappoint or upset the receiver—I'm hard pressed to think of the circumstances under which it's not to your direct benefit to call with no news.

Your Approximate Waiting Time Is . . .

Studies have shown that people mind waiting a lot less when they know how long it's going to be. Evidence of this can be found on countless customer service telephone lines, not to mention in your local subway or bus station. Given this, I recommend including the "approximate waiting time" in your reply to any communication to which you aren't able to give an immediate response.

28 | Keep Current Outside Your Comfort Zone

We all know the importance of keeping current on trends in our own industry. What's often forgotten is the importance of keeping abreast of what's going on in other arenas. But as was discussed in "Adopt a Renaissance Attitude," the well-rounded individual—someone who has the confidence to speak about subjects outside his comfort zone—is the one who stands out in multiple situations.

That said, we don't all have endless hours to stay abreast of what's going on in the world—particularly if we are changing careers, or seeking to solidify our reputation in our current position. For those in either of these circumstances, I offer the following specific suggestions:

If you are seeking a job, you must devote yourself to learning what's new in technology, both in your field and in the world at large. Why? Because a company seeking to hire a new marketing manager, for example, is far more likely—given résumés with comparable experience—to choose the candidate who can not only create and pitch a new marketing strategy, but who also commands the necessary information to articulate to the online team how they can support and enhance the company's new message. And in the same way your car mechanic has greater respect for you if you understand the general workings of your automobile, you will command greater respect from the technology team if you have a basic grasp of their vocabulary.

So what's the easiest, fastest way to keep abreast of what's happening in the field of technology, as it relates to your industry? Change your home page. Many of you spend twenty to thirty minutes there daily, browsing through current articles. Why not take that same time to learn what's new and what's next?

Which pages do I recommend? The website www.kurzweilAI.net offers current events and breaking news in the technology arena, while www.arstechnica.com will put cutting-edge information on trends and capabilities in technology in both the PC and the Mac world in front of you daily. Twenty to thirty minutes spent reading one or two articles from these sites is all that's needed to begin to give you facility with the subject matter.

With this information in hand you are far more qualified to talk to someone about the design of your own website—your shop window to the world during your job search. Familiarity with the subject will help you not only to write the schematic for your designer, but also to hold an informed conversation regarding the possible inclusion of sound, video, or interactive elements.

When you are talking to your possible future employers, you will be able to speak with authority not only about their site, but also about their competition's, enabling, for example—if we return to the example of our hopeful future marketing executive—a conversation along the lines of "I noticed X firm has Y assets (audio/video testimonials/ multiple microsites). I think it would be great if those were added to your site. Do assets of this kind exist or do they need to be produced? If they do, I'd be happy to talk to your online development team about how we can work together to have them created."

All of which sets you up to be their go-to person in multiple situations.

Alternatively, say you've gotten the job in marketing, but now find yourself so immersed in the day-to-day operations of selling your product that it's hard to think bigger picture. In this situation, I would recommend changing your home page to either www.trendwatching .com or www.springwise.com, both of which offer a full-spectrum view of where our interests, technology, and creativity are taking us. With this information in hand, it's far more likely you will be able to formulate a marketing plan that both leverages the technology on which you've gotten up to speed and incorporates the trends that will make your campaign both cutting-edge and memorable.

What you'll likely discover once you do this is the inherent pleasure that comes from being able to speak a new language — and entering a new world.

29 | Have a Scheme (or at Least a Blog)

Even a few years ago, having a personal presence online was seen as at best a luxury and at worst an eccentricity. These days, it's essential. If you can't be Googled, you don't exist. Given this, as you begin to think about technology, it is critical for you—whether you work in a corporate environment or not—to have a blog or personal website of your own; not doing so signals to employers and customers that you are out of touch with modern rhythms.

And lest you think that only companies are online, or that people exclusively discuss "business" there, a recent poll by the blog search engine Technorati that covered almost thirteen hundred bloggers in over sixty countries discovered that 79 percent of people blog about personal interests, 46 percent blog about their industry or profession (but not in an official capacity), and only 12 percent blog on behalf of their companies.

So, let's start with blogs. Before we go any further, we'd better agree on what a blog is: A blog is a Web-based commentary site, usually written in a first-person, conversational manner about just about anything you can imagine, and displayed in reverse chronological order. It can (and I recommend it should) include text, pictures, and links to videos, news items, etc. that interest, annoy, or inspire you. Done well, they offer an incredibly effective yet low-cost way to establish a basic Web presence, to build up your personal brand visibility, and to enhance your credibility. If you run your own business, they're a great way to influence the public "conversation" about your company, gain customer insight, and communicate with the other stakeholders in your business (employees, suppliers, etc.).

How do you get started on a blog? There are a number of free sites to get you started, like http://wordpress.com/, www.blogger.com/, or home.spaces.live.com/. Wiki Blog even has a free eight-step video entitled "How to Start a Blog" available at http://www.wikihow.com/Start-a-Blog.

These sites or others you can find will walk you through the nuts and bolts of the process; here are my thoughts on tone and content:

- Use your own voice—don't write as if there is someone over your shoulder: Authenticity is essential.

- While you should be honest and open, you should also be respectful of your subject and your audiences: no insults, no profanity. Keep criticism to a minimum.

- Link to those who interest or influence you; the more you reference, and have links to and on your blog, the stronger your presence will be within the blogosphere.

- If you're blogging specifically about your business, don't treat blogging like advertising—it's a conversation, not a sermon. For that reason, make sure that you listen and respond to the feedback you receive. Also, don't simply post reviews and/or press releases.

- If you work for a company, and are discussing that industry, find out (and stick to) your company's blogging policy.

- Having your name and your product/company's name in the URL generally means Google will index it higher with respect to rank.

- Once you begin it, it's important to keep it fairly current. I'm not saying you have to update it daily—or even weekly. But I wouldn't let more than two to three weeks go by without saying something.

What keeps people coming back to your blog? Content they can use. The more your blog includes essential/inside information and/or quirky/funny anecdotes they can't get elsewhere, the more likely they are to return.

Once you have your blog established, link it to your LinkedIn, Facebook, MySpace, Twitter, etc. profiles. They all have spaces where URLs can be added to your personal information.

The bigger step is, of course, establishing your own site. This can either be personal or for your business.

How to begin? The first thing to know is that a personal site isn't just a giant blog: You'll need a scheme. Whether you decide to build the site yourself (sites such as www.register.com and www.network solutions.com have templates on hand for this) or have someone build it for you (take a look at www.b2kcorp.com), I recommend starting by writing a schemata: a detailed document that includes every element you want the site to include. As you put this together, it's important to look both at the competition (to make sure there's nothing you're neglecting that appears to be mandatory elsewhere) and at the sites you frequent (which may seem on the surface to have nothing to do with your field, but all of which have features you find compelling), and then ask yourself, "How can I make that work for me?" I would also have you think ahead to what you might not need at the moment, but will want to have later, such as subscription services and video, so you are sure you begin to design something that has the capacity to build out those elements one day.

What elements do I think it's important for every site to include? In my experience, personal sites should include:

- Your bio (This is not a résumé, but a paragraph or two filled with active language that lays out specific details about what you've accomplished, and why others should care.)

- A professional headshot (While I know these can be expensive, they are well worth the money. In my dream world, they're not only professional-looking, they convey your personality, too— there's nothing wrong with smiling. I don't recommend having your arms crossed over your chest, or leaning your chin on your hand, both of which "read" as discomfort.)

- A statement of your goals

- Your contact details

- Links to sites you frequent (Again, the more you include, the better. If these can show a breadth of interests to demonstrate general curiosity, then you really make my heart sing.)

If available, you might also include a portfolio of papers and/or PowerPoint presentations that you've written or executed, photos and/or video of you presenting at conferences, and—perhaps—a mention of one or two general interests. (If you do choose to include these, I will tell you that one of my clients who works in the banking industry told me that banks do look to see if you've played team sports.) If you post samples of your work, make sure you assert copyright by adding a © your name or organization, and the year.

Company sites should have—at minimum:

- Information on how, when, and by whom the company was founded

- A description of its services in terms of the value it delivers to the customer

- A list of personnel with headshots and bios

- A list of frequently asked questions

- A way to ask questions

- Contact information

- Testimonials: either written or video

If you have a list of your core values or a mission statement, do make sure that it not only accurately reflects your company's ethos and character, but that it's written as simply and sensibly as possible: Here's what I do, here's why I do it, here's whom I do it for. I stress this because I've discovered that many people become so overwhelmed when tackling this that they put together something that makes it sound like their work would make the Dalai Lama hang his head in shame for not trying hard enough, and that they're suddenly using a lot of "ten-cent" or "SAT" words to describe that work. In order to be effective, however, it needs to be both believable and memorable—to your constituents as well as your customers. What company mission statements do I like? Goldman Sachs has a very clear outline: http://www2.goldmansachs.com/our-firm/about-us/business-principles. And Patagonia has a simple, convincing statement of its values: http://www.patagonia.com/usa/patagonia.go?assetid=2047&ln=24. If, as you begin to work, you are feeling the need for inspiration, you might look at *101 Mission Statements from Top Companies* by Jeffrey Abrahams.

With regard to design and upkeep, you want to think of your website as your shop window to the world. As with bricks-and-mortar stores, it's worth investing significant time and resources to ensure it's welcoming, is easy to navigate, and provides readers with the essentials. If you can find a way to offer a free "gift with purchase" for coming by—expertise, a quote, inside information: an actual free gift!—so much the better, as, again, this will keep them coming back for more. If you have someone in house who's up to putting together a newsletter that provides readers with valuable industry information/advice/tips, this is a great way to build your customer mailing list. At minimum, it is absolutely vital that if you offer an email address for information or service, you or someone else respond to any queries received in a timely way; it can't be an email box that you check once a month.

To my mind, the best stores are the ones that catch your eye as you go by, that you enter with expectation, and that you leave saying, "I didn't even know I needed this—now I don't know how I lived without it!." With the proper planning, creativity, and upkeep, your blog or website will be the same.

30 | Favor the Moment

Every encounter is an opportunity to strengthen our connections, develop our personal database, burnish our image, and, ultimately, further our dreams. If this feels like an exaggeration, consider the following example: Your client asks you during a routine call if you know of a great restaurant for a networking gathering, and you say, "Not off the top of my head, but let me think about it and get back to you," after which you don't give it another thought. My guess is there's a pretty good chance that when that networking gathering does take place, you won't be included. And while I don't know the exact table over which the seeds of Google were planted, I do know that ideas don't spring into full-fledged, moneymaking behemoths without some discussion—and that they are often catalyzed and nurtured at just such gatherings.

As you can see, I believe that one of the primary ways to build your network is via these small, seemingly insignificant favors, as my experience has been that that they work like compound interest: You don't see their value in the short term, but long term they have the potential for invaluable exponential gains.

"Okay," you may be thinking, "I'm fine with doing the small favors, the follow-up, and the follow through, but what about when I'm asked for large favors? At a time when everyone's value is so indeterminate, isn't it madness to put yourself out for anyone else?"

No, I don't think so. In fact, this is an element of favors that I'd like to do away with: the idea that there should be tangible, measurable reciprocity involved—that the only reason to give is ultimately to get back in kind, or better.

Why is this attitude damaging? It's damaging because it assumes a finite universe, i.e., "If I give someone my good idea or my amazing connection they might steal it, and I will be left with nothing." Really? Are you so poor in ideas that you can't afford to offer one up? Are you so short on charisma that you doubt your ability to maintain your value with the connections you have, or your potential to make new ones?

Do you really think so little of your potential?

If so, here's how you need to begin thinking about it:

As those of you who have been on diets know, it's only a matter of time before your body notices you're not giving it as much food as you used to, and so it lowers your basal metabolism rate and suddenly your ability to drop weight is significantly decreased—you started hoarding, so your body started hoarding. I think the same is true of your brain: When you start hoarding then your brain starts hoarding, and then where are you? In starvation.

You need to keep your mental metabolism high. One way to do this is by doing favors for others. What kind of favors am I talking about? Well, one of the things I make a practice of doing—and request my clients make a habit of as well—is looking through my address book at least once a month and thinking about ways in which two of my unrelated connections might find a way to work together. For example, I recently put together my friend Alice, who is starting her own cosmetics line, with my friend Kelly, whose background is in packaging and design: a series of three short phone calls that resulted not only in my being able to spend time with two people I like and respect, but also in their finding a way to do business together. It was an easy favor on my part that—while there is no tangible future reward—keeps my networking metabolism high.

Another favor I make a practice of is giving free consultations to those who can't afford my fees—particularly college-aged kids. Why kids? After all, it's unlikely that particular demographic is going to be able to give back in kind anytime soon. Well, that's precisely why. A lot of people were incredibly kind about giving me advice and counsel when I was starting out. Am I so important now that I can't pay it forward? Not likely. And in fact, these sessions give back to me a hundredfold, as I find college students' enthusiasm so contagious, and their way of looking at the world so novel, that I end up tackling my own work with greater energy and fresh perspectives.

The flip side, of course, to doing favors for others is learning how to ask others to do favors for you—something many of us are uncomfortable doing. Perhaps that's because we think it makes us look inefficient, or weak; or perhaps we worry about being able to respond in kind; or perhaps we don't want to "owe anybody anything." But leaders as disparate as Machiavelli and Benjamin Franklin point to the wisdom of asking others for favors. Machiavelli said, "He who gives up his own convenience for the convenience of others, only loses his own," and Franklin opined, "If you want to make a friend, let someone do you a favor."

I think both make solid points. As Machiavelli notes, the only person you hurt by not asking is yourself; while Benjamin Franklin asks you to consider that asking favors of others is a way to draw them to you, to get them invested in your success. From where I sit, the key to it is to be smart about how you ask.

How can you ensure this?

First: pick your person wisely. Don't reach out helter-skelter to anyone or everyone. People need to know you approached *them* specifically, for a good reason, so when you make your request, be sure that reason is articulated: Is it because of their expertise, their accomplishments, their business acumen? Be specific.

Second: Don't drop it on them unexpectedly. No one wants to get blindsided at breakfast, lunch, cocktails, or dinner—in person at all, in fact. Instead, I recommend sending an email letting them know you would like to talk to them about their doing you a favor (use those words—don't beat around the bush) and asking them if they would be willing to speak with you about it further via telephone or in person.

Third: Both in your note and when you speak, be sure to tell them you don't expect an immediate response—that you want them to take time to think about it—and that you will be comfortable with whatever their decision ends up being. (Please note: if you can't say that in all honesty, don't ask the favor. They don't owe you anything—if you feel like they do, you're already in murky waters.)

For example, in writing this book, there were any number of times I needed "expert witness testimony" on a subject or industry with which I wasn't familiar. In every case, the note I wrote to the person in question spelled out the thought process that had brought me to them, exactly what I needed from them, how I planned to use the information I was given, and an offer to let them vet my final copy to make sure I had understood what I was told, and closed with "With thanks for any help you can give." In every case, the response I received was enthusiastic, offered far more information than I'd even thought to ask for, and arrived with kind, encouraging words as well—and our follow-up conversations were equally collegial. In fact, what I discovered—and I think you will discover too—is that, approached respectfully, people are generally more than happy to help.

Both the doing and the asking of favors is an important part of intelligent business—an alternate "currency" you can use to achieve your ends. And, just like cash, used wisely, invested well, and spent thriftily, they will earn you extraordinary rewards over time.

Return Receipt Requested

Just as important as doing favors for other people is the acknowledgment of favors others have done for you. For example, if a friend makes an email introduction, provides a referral, or offers their advice, it is critical—*regardless of the outcome*—to take the time to thank him or her for their intention and efforts. When doing so, my request would be that you pick up the phone. Sending an email is adequate, but who wants to be known as being adequate?

Additionally, it's important to be respectful of the time and/or professional constraints of the person doing the favor: Be on time, have your questions prepared, don't press for "inside" information, and thank them promptly for their help—regardless of how useful you might have found it. Remember that your behavior when you "cash in" the favor is a direct reflection on the person who made the introduction. Don't embarrass them—or yourself—by showing up as less than your best self.

31 | Brain Barter

Last spring my friend Karen and I were sitting around plotting our world domination (as one does) and came up with the idea of a networking group called Brain Barter. Our thought was that in this economy it was critical to have access to lots of areas of expertise, and that introducing the smart, well-connected people we knew to one another couldn't hurt. In the year since the group's founding we have grown from two to more than one hundred fifty, and the advice, connections, and camaraderie we have given one another have been invaluable—with everything from website-design help to frequent-flier miles, public speaking training to eyeglass frames, legal advice to architectural input being freely handed around. The only mandatory criteria we have for joining is that your first question be "How can I help you?"

Why is this story useful to you? My hope is that it will spur you to step back from your standard approach to networking—which I imagine focuses on making contacts—and take a look at what skills and/or expertise you have that could be valuable to others. Yes, we will remain a cash-based economy—we're not switching over to wampum anytime soon—but trading skills and services is smart, if for no other reason than to give you a sense of the value of your training and knowledge. And while I know it can be uncomfortable to bring up the idea of "barter," it's a system that worked for thousands of years before the current one was devised, is still used in many parts of the world, and, frankly, doesn't have the potential to break down with the same kind of catastrophic results as ours does.

So, how to begin? My suggestion would be to sit down with one or two friends who have a wealth of knowledge about something you've always wanted to know about, but haven't yet had the time or inclination to learn—whether it's landscape gardening, building a PowerPoint deck, or designing a closet—and tell them frankly how much you admire their expertise. I would then ask them if there's anything that you do that they have always wanted to find out more about. While the answer for this might seem self-evident (especially if you have a string of letters after your name proclaiming your expertise in an arena), it's possible you'll also get some answers that surprise you, because we all have talents we so take for granted that we no longer even think of them as talents—they're just what we do, or something we've learned about but consider a hobby, and therefore not worth much.

But these talents can be gold—or, at least, worth their weight in gold. If, for example, you have a friend who's made a hobby of gardening, having that person come put in a vegetable or flower garden has the potential not only to feed your family, but also to increase the value of your home, once your perfectly manicured flower beds are in place. Your friend, in turn, might prize your ability to turn a phrase, and might ask you to review his marketing copy, website schemata, and the like, all of which have the potential to increase his revenue. (With regard to keeping the barter "even," I suggest keeping a log of hours spent and make sure that stays equal, as you never want others to feel you've taken advantage of them.)

If you're feeling ambitious enough to want to start a group of your own, there are a number of factors it's helpful to keep in mind. One is to (to the best of your ability) make sure that when friends bring friends, they bring people at your peer level. This ensures that everyone leaves feeling they've both added and been given value. Second, declare that this list of contacts is off-limits for any other kind of solicitation; if what's on the table is not for barter but for sale, then use another list. And finally, the most important piece of advice I can offer is to ensure that those who join are as anxious to give as they are to receive. This is the only way we've found to guarantee that everyone leaves feeling they've gotten the most for their smarts.

The Elegant Extrication

Every now and then you'll find yourself trapped in the corner at a networking event talking and talking to someone from whom you want to step away, but have no idea how to do so without being abrupt or discourteous. In these situations I recommend the following: "I'm so glad we had the chance to meet. Since our time tonight is limited—and I know there are other people you want to talk to—may I get your card and follow up with you this week? Is email best or shall I just give you a call?" The beauty of this is that you've made their time a priority, which ensures they save face, and extricated yourself so you can maximize yours.

(As a general note, my request is that you follow up with everyone from whom you take a card—no exceptions—if only to say "It was so nice to meet you." A useful website for help with this is www .shoeboxed.com, which allows you to scan and organize business cards rather than keeping them in the proverbial shoebox.)

Stop the Bombing

One of the more common missteps I see at networking events is a tendency to establish credibility by letting others know whom you know, rather than what you do. This name-dropping often sounds like "So, you design handbags?" "Yes—you may have seen X carrying it in the recent issue of *People*. She's such a good friend." Or, "So, you're a writer?" "I am. X, Y, and Z have all endorsed my books. We've known each other for years."

The trouble with this follow-up is that you've now moved the conversation away from how your business/product/service might improve the life of the person you're speaking with; instead, he's in a conversation about your Rolodex—a topic he's unlikely to find as interesting.

How can you establish your credibility without putting others off—particularly if you do have significant connections? My suggestion would be to find a way to link the life of the person in question to the connection you know—so you might say, "Yes, I design handbags that are particularly popular with working mothers, as my bags have the capacity for both computers and kid paraphernalia. Do you have kids?" From there, it's easy enough to work in your well-known chum who's also a working mom.

In addition to overt name-dropping, I also caution my clients about having too many "best friends," as there's something equally disquieting about meeting people who—no matter whom you mention—respond by announcing they've been best friends with that person since they met in the paddling pool. My request is that you concentrate instead on making the person with whom you're speaking feel like he or she is the most important person in your life.

Make Expectations Explicit

It's impossible to network effectively if half your mind is occupied with the fact that your partner is outraged that you are once again missing family dinner to go—in their mind—socialize. For this reason, I strongly recommend that in the same way you make your expectations explicit to your employees so they can organize their time, you make your expectations explicit to your family so they can organize theirs. The idea that you have to "present yourself" properly to your family may seem counterintuitive—they're your family, after all; can't they see you're doing this for *them*? But the fact remains that telling your loved ones up front that, until financial calm is achieved, you will essentially be working six days a week is a smart way to start a conversation about how you all can best enjoy the seventh.

One way to do this is to designate a particular day or family activity "untouchable"—at our house this was dinner on Sunday night. Having this "written in stone" means that when there is the occasional slip—maybe a flight schedule means you really can't keep your promise that week—everybody has the same jumping-off place for the renegotiation.

A common pitfall in such situations is that when hard workers do unexpectedly have some free time, they sometimes expect their family members to equally joyfully drop everything to accommodate the unexpected break in their schedule. When this isn't possible, everyone can end up feeling grumpy: The hard worker feels aggrieved that his gesture is not appreciated, and the people to whom the gesture is being made see the attempt as just a different species of selfishness. If you find yourself in either party, consider the intent of the gesture, and strive to show respect for other people's schedules as well as your own. And, of course, remember that to a fifth-grader, his school concert is just as big a deal to him as a presentation to the CEO is to you.

32 | Build an Advisory Board

CPR requests that before you begin trying to resuscitate someone you look out into the crowd, pick one person, point at him or her, and say, "*YOU* call 911." The reason for this is that when we're in an emergency we often think others are as invested as we are in its urgency—and in helping. But often they're not. They're just rubbernecking.

I've found the same can be true when you come to a crossroad in your career. Almost inevitably a crowd will gather, filled with ideas and opinions and advice. The tricky bit is teasing out which of these people—and which of their comments—you should pay attention to, and which can be discounted as psychic rubbernecking; which might be a well-meaning citizen who will nevertheless "move the body without stabilizing the spine" and which is an actual career EMS technician.

Why is this important? It's important because no matter the size of your company—multimillion-dollar and worldwide, or you sitting in your sweatpants in front of your laptop—you need to have an advisory board: a group of trusted people whose expertise you value, whose opinions are objective, and who, frankly, push you farther than you would have gone on your own.

I've flagged these attributes for a number of reasons. I chose the word "expertise" rather than "reputation" because it forces you to consider the actual nuts and bolts of the questions you are going to ask, and the potential advice you might be given. It's easy to say, "Oh, I definitely want to ask so-and-so CEO to be on my board," but if you can't articulate the specifics of *why*—other than that you feel it would burnish your reputation—then how are you going to approach him in such a way that he actually consents to do it? You also need to be able to identify for whomever you approach exactly what *they* will be gaining by being part of your venture (the invaluable "What's their egg?" theory from *How to Wow*). How is your success likely to contribute to their success? How is your company's newly formed reputation going to enhance theirs?

The other thing to think about when you consider expertise is the importance of choosing people with complementary—or even vastly different—skill sets. For example, my advisory board not only includes various people who are well versed in the world of media, it also has members who are fonts of wisdom on cutting-edge technology, design, and online marketing, as these are areas in which I'm neither an expert nor likely to become one anytime soon. Having this pool of knowledge standing by has meant that when I have been unexpectedly confronted by needing to put together a proposal for a client in twenty-four hours, I've been able to send over a package whose presentation enhances what I have to offer; or that when I've wanted to test-drive marketing to a new constituency, I haven't had to start pulling together information from scratch.

The reason I articulate the value of finding people who are objective is that it can be all too easy to surround yourself with sycophants, or just well-intentioned friends who want you to succeed. While I think it's critical to have people who believe in you, and in the potential of your idea, you also want to be sure they're willing to ask you the hard questions and hold you accountable before something disastrous happens (because the last thing you want to hear in that moment is "Well, I always was dubious about the wisdom of that idea").

Finally, I think it's critical to have a few people who push you way outside your comfort zone. My friend Karen specifically keeps one person on her board who has "champagne and caviar" tastes, despite the fact that she usually has a "hamburger" budget. What's his value? Well, although thirteen of the fifteen ideas he brings to the table are not possible, there are always at least two that, with a little creativity, can be incorporated—elements that end up taking her work to a whole new level.

And while this is not mandatory, the ideal board will include people who have known you for varying degrees of time. The reason for this is that if you reach out only to people who've known you for years, it's possible you'll end up in any number of conversations along the lines of "Well, remember when you were working at X and Y happened? You don't want to repeat that scenario." Alternatively, having a group that's only known you since you became bright, shiny, and new doesn't give you the valuable institutional memory that can be gained by having at least one person who knows your foibles.

Having targeted your candidates, the next thing to think about is how to go about requesting their participation. Again, this is a balancing act. You don't want to make it so informal that they feel you aren't taking them, or yourself, seriously. Alternatively, you don't want to make it so formal that they begin to get anxious about the commitment involved. Additionally, it's likely you will have varying degrees of familiarity with each potential participant, which will impact how you ask them.

With this in mind, I would approach those you know well with a certain degree of formality, as it will help them understand the gravity with which you are beginning your new venture. Simply saying to an old friend over lunch, "Hey, you want to be on my advisory board?" is unlikely to make her take the request—or you—seriously. That said, I do think lunch is a fine way to broach the conversation. I would just take the time to set it up carefully: When you issue the invitation, tell people that it's for a specific project you'd like to discuss with them. With regard to specifying exactly why you thought their contribution would be valuable, don't assume they know. It's rare that most of us sit down with our close friends and say, "Hey, I really admire the way you do X, Y, or Z," but this is critical for them to hear in this situation if they are going to approach their role with enthusiasm.

With regard to approaching those you don't know that well, I think a phone call is always the best way to begin, as it's important for them to hear your tone—particularly if they might have concerns about why you're calling. If you don't get them on the phone, leave a message saying you have an opportunity you'd like to discuss with them and telling them you'll follow up with an email requesting a specific appointment time. Once you have the appointment, as noted, begin with the specifics of why you are making this request of them, and tell them exactly how much of their time you think it will involve. Be sure to let them know that you don't expect an immediate answer—that you're happy to have them think about it for as long as is necessary.

With those you know not at all, I recommend a formal, snail mail letter outlining the objective of your company, exactly why you are contacting them and nobody else, and what becoming involved is likely to do for them. Again, you will need to include the specifics of the time commitment and to mention the option to spend some time considering your proposal.

Much of this may seem like make-work—why not just reach out to people on an ad hoc basis when you're looking for a specific answer? The reason is that that approach doesn't validate their experience, or acknowledge their generosity in contributing to your work. Additionally, having a group of people who have been approached in an official capacity means that they're more likely to be thinking of you and your company's future in an ongoing way, netting you greater rewards as you go from strength to strength.

33 | Don't Ask Permission

Every New Year's Eve, instead of picking a resolution for the year, I pick a motto: a mental bumper sticker that will exemplify how I will move through the world over the coming twelve months. Recently, that slogan was "Don't Ask Permission." It's no coincidence that with that slogan driving me, I sat down and wrote *How to Wow*.

I mention this because it's possible some of you are reading here about starting your own business, building advisory boards, positioning yourself for a promotion, founding your own networking group, etc., and thinking, "Oh, but I could never do that—that's just not me."

Really? Who says?

And please don't think I write the above lightly. I had a nine-to-five job for years and never imagined I could leave; in fact, I was quite strident about how I needed structure, how happy I was being my boss's go-to girl, how important I felt it was to have the freedom outside my day job to pursue multiple interests.

But life hands you many challenges and opportunities (or, as we call them in yoga, AFGOs: another freakin' growth opportunity). In my case, media training caught my interest at the same time my frustration with my current career was at its peak. Although I could tell you my decision to leave was well thought out, I'd be fibbing.

I was pissed.

I quit.

I was terrified.

I was liberated.

Over the course of the (very sharp) learning curve that followed, what I discovered was that I did love structure, but I could create my own. I did love being the go-to girl, but I didn't need to confine myself to being that for only one person. I did need to pursue multiple interests, but now the only person I had to answer to about when, where, and why was me.

I also discovered any number of people who said, "But what makes you qualified?" and "Are you sure you don't just want to go back to your old job? Better safe than sorry."

But here's what I learned: You can't wait for someone else to tell you you're qualified. After you leave school, no one is handing out diplomas saying, "Marketing Manager," "Executive Coach," "Entrepreneur," "Writer," or "CEO." Additionally, as we've learned in the past year, there's very little in this world that's safe. It is, however, very easy to end up being sorry—and sorry usually comes from regret: regret that you didn't trust yourself, that you didn't back your own talent, that you didn't push yourself to the limit of your potential.

And despite the fact that Kenneth Lay, of Enron fame, and then infamy, is quoted as having chosen "Anything's possible" as his motto, I do want you to embrace that mind-set. Anything is possible once you decide you're willing to work for it; what other people think about your choice is none of your business.

If this sounds selfish to you, I'd ask you to consider the following: It is extremely difficult for people who are profoundly unhappy or unfulfilled themselves to make others—even those they love—happy. While there is an obvious balance to be struck, in some ways you owe it to those you love to become who you are.

It's my intention that the habits outlined here give you the mental stamina to tackle anything you'd like to succeed in; that the knowledge offered here gives you the confidence to look forward to any interview, meeting, or presentation you participate in; and that the practices delineated here allow you to move up your own learning curve with ease. If you've read this far, you are now primed to take the world by storm. My friend David has a tattoo on his arm that says, in Latin, "Put that down and get to work." I went a less dramatic route, with a bracelet that has inscribed on it, "Your work is to dis-cover your work, and then with all your heart to give yourself to it."

You choose your work—and your worth. You decide who you are—then become who you are. Your success is there for the taking. Don't ask permission.

Summing It Up:

- It's infinitely possible to "plan for courage": High-stakes meetings, interviews, and activities become far easier when you can point to concrete steps (such as the seemingly mundane checklist) that you've taken to ensure your success.

- When searching for a job, applying a "Do It, Delegate It, or Delete It" policy to any request that comes in verbally, telephonically, or electronically enables you to follow up, and follow through, with greater efficiency.

- Having a "Thick Face"—attending interviews for the purposes of practicing your answers, floating your ideas, and collecting additional data—can help to hone your presentation and negotiation skills.

- Taking the time to (gracefully) put yourself, either on paper or in person, in the sight line of the person pulling the trigger on an important decision is one more way you can help to guarantee your success.

- Calling with no news—becoming known as someone who picks up the phone to follow through, regardless of whether or not you have the required, or desired, information in hand—is critical to building others' trust.

- Keeping abreast of current technology by changing your home page to kurzweilAI.net or arstechnica.com ensures you can

speak with authority about the possibilities for implementing
your ideas.

- A personal presence online, either with a blog or a website, is
  essential. Having this virtual shop window up and running
  reassures employers and customers that you are in touch with
  modern rhythms; enhances your reputation; and builds your
  customer database.

- Doing favors for others is one way to keep your mental
  metabolism high. Accepting favors from others is an effective
  way to get them invested in your success.

- Bartering your skills and smarts is an effective way to gauge your
  own, and leverage others', expertise, connections, and talent.

- Putting together an advisory board—a group of trusted people
  whose expertise you value, and whose opinions are objective—is
  critical to developing the network you need, keeping the
  momentum you require, and maintaining the perspective that's
  fundamental to ensuring your success.

- You can't wait for someone else to tell you you're qualified. You
  choose your work—and your worth. You decide who you are—
  then become who you are. Your success is there for the taking.
  Don't ask permission.

Remain Calm and Carry On:
An Afterword

Every New Year's Eve I make a practice of choosing a slogan that embodies my attitude for the year ahead. A few years ago that slogan was, "Don't ask permission." The thought behind it is you can't wait for people to tell you you're good enough, creative enough, educated enough, smart enough. You decide these things then demonstrate they are true—you are the only person whose permission is needed to become your best self.

This past year I chose, "I'll see that and raise you." As many of you know this is a phrase used in poker when you're willing to take your bet to the next level. Little did I know when I picked it how often I would return to it as a rallying cry, for 2009 was a year riddled with all-time highs and lows: for every success a health issue, for every friendship gained a bizarre betrayal, and for every friend who realized their dream of a son or daughter, the unexpected death of a dearly beloved.

It seems the universe took me at my word.

As I write, I'm thinking many of you had a similar year: a roller-coaster ride composed of both breathless anticipation interspersed with high-energy delight and low-grade dread interspersed with adrenaline-surging fear.

The hodgepodge of what it means to be human.

As I walked around this year—feeling my feelings—I initially found myself chanting the following impromptu mantra: "Don't freak out, don't freak out, don't freak out . . ."

But then it struck me—why was I speaking in the negative? The same way using "crisis" makes everyone involved act more peculiar, using the phrase "freak out" was going to make me more peculiar. (Not to mention that any sentence beginning with "Don't" is sure to ratchet up your blood pressure.)

Consequently, I flipped my internal monologue to the slogan adopted by the British in WWII: "Remain calm and carry on."

Ah. I could breathe again.

Another thing that has helped me breathe more deeply is the unstinting support so many of you have shown the Wow-World.

A number of you sent in questions that sparked the essays found on the next few pages: "Don't Get Flustered, Get Factual" was the result of job interview scenarios that ranged from peculiar to preposterous; "How to Wow Like Pretty Woman" was an advisory I wrote based on your stories of various client capers; "Feels Like (Virtual) Team Spirit" was a response to a growing shift to worldwide teams—and the subsequent need for building trust and efficiency in these environments.

Additionally, many of you sent extraordinarily kind, encouraging letters. These have provided marvelous ballast and fuel for my remaining calm and carrying on, and I thank you for them—so very much.

As you head into this new decade, I hope you discover the slogan that offers you the mental sustenance you need to make your days both prosperous and joyful.

And if there is any ballast, or fuel, I can provide for you, please don't hesitate to get in touch.

With gratitude and joy,
Frances

Don't Get Flustered, Get Factual

There appears to be an epidemic of inappropriateness pervading the job interview world these days. Several people I know have gotten questions that left them, literally, speechless—and one wasn't so much disconcerted by a question as by the manner in which it was asked.

The following are a few suggestions I made for how each of them might have responded. If any of you have additional ideas, I'd love to hear them. (Alternatively, if you've been asked anything, or experienced anything, that left you confounded, I'd love to hear those stories, too.)

Q: "Do you know the average age of the people who work in this company?"

This was a question an older client of mine got when she applied for a position in a very youthful organization. While I can only speculate about what the interviewer's intention might have been, I can tell you the result was that my client was left feeling shamed for even applying.

How did I recommend she handle this kind of leading question?

Leading questions demand fact-based responses. You don't want to get into what you think your questioner is after, or do the dirty work of negating something that hasn't been overtly stated.

Consequently, my Monday-morning quarterback coaching to her was to respond, "I do."

Q: "You realize you're going to need to ugly up if you get this job."

This leading question was asked of one of my, admittedly, extraordinarily beautiful clients. As always, we could only speculate about the questioner's intention—though I have to say we both found the pigtail-pulling undertone distinctly . . . underwhelming.

In this instance, again, I didn't want her to do the troublemaker's dirty work for him. Consequently, my 20/20 hindsight recommendation was to go with the factual, "I don't understand what you're saying."

Admittedly, thinking on your feet when you're asked these types of questions isn't easy, but if you can keep your answer short, sweet, and fact-based, you're likely to disconcert your questioner as much as he or she has disconcerted you.

Finally, one of my clients went into an interview during which, in her words, "The interviewer turned his back to me throughout the interview and asked his questions while looking out the window."

How did I recommend she handle it? Well, calling him on his behavior was going to end in a lose/lose. His reaction was unlikely to be positive, her outcome was therefore likely to be negative. Consequently, I suggested saying, "I find it hard to answer your questions without being able to see your face. May I ask you to turn around, or may I join you at the window?"

What makes this statement powerful is that she takes the onus on herself—it's not that he's being difficult, it's that she finds it tricky to talk to someone who refuses to look at her. Also, it reminds him that her goal is to be her best self in every situation, no matter how difficult.

And, as I'm sure you've discovered, if we can be our best selves—regardless of the circumstances—not only do we wow others, we wow ourselves: the ultimate challenge.

How to Wow Like Pretty Woman

I'm guessing many of you read the above title and thought a) I was joking or b) I've gone off my rocker. Neither is the case. Today we're focusing on what we can all learn from the escort system.

As many of you may remember from seeing *Pretty Woman*, Julia Roberts did not arrive at Richard Gere's door and begin speaking about her other clients. In fact, the producers of the movie went to great lengths to present her as a hooker with a heart of gold—after all, how many of us are so concerned about appearing bright, shiny, and new that we travel with our own dental floss on dates?

But I digress: This post is not about dental hygiene. Instead I want to talk about the wisdom inherent in not talking to one client about another—not saying how busy your other clients are keeping you, how irritating you may find them, how happy you are to have completed their project.

I mean, who wants an escort who shows up and says, "I'm *so* sorry I'm late—my last appointment took forever."

So as you move through your hectic holiday season—a time when many of your clients are likely wanting 110 percent of your attention, while giving you 50 percent of their own—don't forget the importance of being a good escort. As far as they are concerned, each client with whom you deal should feel like they are the only one in your life.

Feels Like (Virtual) Team Spirit

With more and more companies using the latest technology to find efficiencies in the recession, far-flung, "virtual" teams are becoming a part of many people's work day. Therefore, I thought it was important to put together a top-ten list of the most effective strategies for building and maintaining virtual team spirit—the spirit that builds trust and encourages concrete results.

1. **Gather 'round and go around**
   We all know a picture is worth a thousand words, so sharing pictures of team members is critical. Still more valuable is posting them on a one-sheet diagram of a clock face so members can say, "This is Ellen at nine o'clock," thereby saving team members from having to scroll frantically through members' pictures to remind themselves who's speaking. This

method counteracts disembodied voices on conference calls and helps prevent "hiding" by participants.

2. **One may be lonely, but it's also the most effective number**
On conference calls, if even one member of the team is in an office by him- or herself, the remainder of the team needs to be separated from one another—even if they are in the same offices. This can seem like a pain to arrange, but anything else leaves the person working solo feeling still more isolated.

3. **Sort through the holidays and ho-downs**
If your team is international, building trust is about more than the time zone in which they're located. Many countries celebrate different holidays, start work later, stay longer, etc. Additionally, some Asian countries have a policy of working on Saturdays that needs to be acknowledged and factored in at the outset. If you work this out in advance, you can even gain efficiency by working out the ideal schedule for "handover" of work.

4. **Establish your "note-passing" policy**
The same way it is distracting to a teacher and fellow students to have two people passing notes in class, it is distracting for two people to be IM'ing or emailing during a call. (And please don't think others don't notice. They do.) My recommendation is that the only use of IM or email during a call would be to alert others to a technical breakdown.

5. **Version 2.WHAT?**
Few things are more maddening than scrolling through six versions of a document—each with a very slightly different draft name—trying to figure out who touched it last. My suggestion is begin with V.01, for version 1, and move on from there. This will, at least, take you through V.99 before you need to

recalibrate. A great add-on is to adopt the protocol that "whole numbered versions" (e.g. V2.0) are "client-ready," whereas fractional numbers (e.g. V0.23) are still works in progress.

6. **Show your work**
Should you make any change in a document that has the potential to be misconstrued (i.e. anything beyond fixing typos/grammar/clarity) include a note explaining the rationale behind the change. This will either mollify team members or give you a jumping off place for discussion—rather than dissension—at your next meeting.

7. **Standardize your team turnaround time or state your "by when"**
People wait far more patiently if they know by when something is going to happen—this is the reason most mass transit has begun incorporating announcements regarding where the next bus/train is, and when it can be expected. Have a stated turnaround time for your team. If that deadline is going to be missed, state by when you will be in touch.

8. **Silence is not (necessarily) golden**
Too often a question is asked and falls into silence, leaving the questioner wondering, "Are they quiet because they agree with me, disagree with me, or are not paying attention to me?" Establish your silence policy—i.e. silence signals disagreement; or each question must be met with a round of polling—explicit yes's or no's from all participants.

9. **"Don't you put that sheep on my head"**
Different countries have different idiomatic expressions—the above was a striking reinterpretation of "Don't try to pull the wool over my eyes." Alternatively, ideas we "run up the flagpole" or consider "a home run," may be similarly misconstrued by

listeners in different countries. Clarify and/or (for fun) keep a running list everyone can learn from. (nb: Poland uses "I wouldn't bet my head on that" for "I wouldn't bet my life"; and one of my favorites is the Italian equivalent of "You can't have your cake and eat it, too": "You can't have a full bottle of wine and a drunk wife.")

10. **Mix it up**

With far-flung teams, there is no opportunity to blow off steam together after work—yet the interpersonal connections forged during these get-togethers is vital to creating camaraderie. What to do? Arrange a weekly test-drive (and subsequent commentary on) the "libation of your nation"—beer, chai, sake, double espresso, or create a signature drink particular to your team alone.

Website Roundup

All websites links can also be viewed at **www.thewowfactor-thebook.com**.

"I Wondered Where That Was. . . ."
www.gothamorganizers.com professional office and home organizers

Home Office Professionalism
www.stamps.com information on online postage accounts
www.pitneyworks.com informatian on personal postage machines
www.efax.com information on free faxing
www.alibaba.com countdown clocks for big projects

Adopt a Renaissance Attitude
http://news.bbc.co.uk BBC News home page
**http://entertainment.timesonline.co.uk/tol/arts_and_entertainment/
   the_tls/** Times Literary Supplement home page
www.metmuseum.org Metropolitan Museum home page
http://www.arlingtoninstitute.org/ Arlington Institute ("committed to
   thinking about global futures and trying to influence rapid, positive
   change") home page
http://www.wfs.org/ World Future Society home page
www.teach12.com The Teaching Company: college and high school
   courses available on DVD

See the Whole Board; Think Several Moves Deep
www.zoomerang.com helps you create your own focus groups
www.surveymonkey.com helps you create your own focus groups

Corporate CliffsNotes
http://harvardbusiness.org Harvard Business School case studies

"If I Only Had X Back at My Office . . ."

www.gotomypc.com service that allows you to log in to your home machine and hard drive from any browser in the world and pick up your confidential documents

Business Class Is About More Than the Salted Almonds

www.prioritypass.com membership in business class lounges around the world

Master the Medium

www.register.com buy your name/business name as a dot.com
www.networksolutions.com buy your name/business names as a dot.com

Eye Spy

www.dictionary.com sign up for its free Word of the Day
www.wordsmith.org another terrific vocabulary enhancement/free Word. A. Day site

Human Resources: An Insider's Guide

www.acethecase.com case interview preparation
www.quintcareers.com/case_interviews.html case interview preparation
www.mckinsey.com/careers/how_do_i_apply/how_to_do_well_in_the _interview.aspx video case interviews you can watch

You Must Have the Cattle

www.aphorisms-galore.info aphorisms for presentations, newsletters, speeches
www.thehypertexts.com epigrams for presentations, newsletters, speeches

Now You're Speaking My Language

www.theladders.com listings for jobs that pay over $100,000 a year.

Research Roundup

www.hoovers.com business reports and profiles on companies nationwide, plus terrific, free "webinars" on numerous business topics
www.charlesschwab.com stock reports on companies nationwide

Keep Current Outside Your Comfort Zone

www.kurzweilAI.net current events and breaking news in the technology arena

www.arstechnica.com cutting-edge information on trends and capabilities in technology in both the PC and Mac worlds

www.trendwatching.com cutting-edge marketing trends

www.springwise.com full-spectrum view of where our interests, technology, and creativity are taking us

Have a Scheme (or at Least a Blog)

http://wordpress.com/ start your own blog

www.blogger.com/ start your own blog

home.spaces.live.com/. start your own blog

http://www.wikihow.com/Start-a-Blog eight-step video on starting your own blog

www.register.com website templates

www.networksolutions.com website templates

www.activedomain.com website templates

www.b2kcorp.com off-site resource for building your website

The Elegant Extrication

www.shoeboxed.com scan and organize your receipts and business cards

Recommended Reading

101 Philosophy Problems, by Martin Cohen, Routledge, 2001.

The Brain That Changes Itself, by Norman Doidge, MD, Penguin, 2007.

Critical Thinking: Tools for Taking Charge of Your Professional and Personal Life, by Richard Paul and Linda Elder, FT Press, 2002.

Eats, Shoots & Leaves, by Lynne Truss, Gotham Books, Penguin Group, Inc., 2004.

(Its children's edition is also great: *Eats, Shoots & Leaves: Why, Commas Really Do Make a Difference!* by Lynne Truss, G.P. Putnam's Sons, 2006).

The Economist Style Guide, Profile Books, 2005.

The Elements of Style, Fourth Edition, by William Strunk, Jr., and E. B. White, Macmillan Publishing Co., 1972.

Emily Post's Etiquette, 17th Edition, by Peggy Post, Collins Living, 2004.

The Intellectual Devotional series, by David S. Kidder and Noah D. Oppenheim, Rodale Books, 2006.

Miss Manners' Guide to Excruciatingly Correct Behavior, Freshly Updated, by Judith Martin and Gloria Kamen, W.W. Norton & Co, 2005.

On Writing, by Stephen King, Pocket Books, 2002.

Pocket Fowler's Modern English Usage, by Robert Allen, Oxford Paperback Reference, 2008.

Robert's Rules in Plain English: A Readable, Authoritative, Easy-to-Use Guide to Running Meetings, 2nd Edition, by Doris P. Zimmerman, Collins, 2005.

Robert's Rules of Order Newly Revised in Brief, by Henry M. Robert III, William J. Evans, Daniel H. Honemann, and Thomas J. Balch, Da Capo Press, 2004.

Thinkertoys: A Handbook of Creative-Thinking Techniques, by Michael Michalko, Ten Speed Press, 2006.

Ultimate Visual Dictionary, Dorling Kindersley Limited, DK Publishing, 2006.

PHOTO: © COSIMO SCIANNA

FRANCES COLE JONES founded Cole Media Management in 1997. From the beginning, the company's focus has been on cultivating clients' inherent strengths to develop the communication skills that will enhance their professional and personal performance. The scope of Jones's work includes preparation for television and print interviews, IPO road shows, meetings with potential investors, and internal meetings with partners, sales staff, and in-house personnel. She also provides presentation skills seminars and speechwriting. The author of *How to Wow*, Frances Cole Jones lives in New York City.

www.thewowfactor-thebook.com
www.howtowow-thebook.com

FRANCES COLE JONES is available for select readings and lectures. To inquire about a possible appearance, please visit www.rhspeakers.com or call 212-572-2013.